C0-CZY-062

Christmas 2005
For Jennifer & Remington Bullock
Have a wonderful Christmas &
Bright 2006. Great having you
for friends, hope
to see more of
you & plan
activities
we like
Love &
Light,
the author

STREAMS
OF THE
SOUL

CRAIG CARPENTER DOWNER

PublishAmerica
Baltimore

First printing

ISBN: 1-4137-7715-5
PUBLISHED BY PUBLISHAMERICA, LLLP
www.publishamerica.com
Baltimore

Printed in the United States of America

TABLE OF CONTENTS

The Tartar. Young, wild bachelor stallion, southern Pine Nut
Range, western Nevada. (1970s).

PERSONA AND REINCARNATION

THE TARTAR: A PERSONA (JANUARY 1996)

Once I was one
of those hated Tartar hordes
  —but I spoke great, flowing poetry, indeed!
And my mind, my tongue,
  was like my sword:
cutting ever so sharply,
  —swiftly to the Truth!
And as forth I did ride
  upon my galloping steed,
something in my very soul
  was freed!
As with one emerging out
  of some unbearable Aftermath,
of Sin's smothering Darkness
  unto the Saving Heavenly Light
that dawned both Within, Without,
  as ever I rode on!
As one called back
  to ever loftier, conscious states,
strangely reminiscent of times
  before some cosmic Fall.
And so as I would ride onward—so daringly!—
  God's very inspiring messages
would set me free!
  Precious and life-sustaining gifts for sure these!
Embodied even in the very pace and cadence
  of —this!— my gloriously powerful
and well-directed steed,
  one who sensed the messages too, indeed!
And in all the strange, weird, new places,

and in all the marvelous times
each without precedence
and that like music onward dashed,
as in all the wondrously distinctive beings
—Oh! Uniquely precious souls and cosmic threads each!—
so a further transcending lesson took its shape!
And Glorious Freedom was our example!
And our message,
one with the freedom,
to all whom we met,
as theirs to us,
both given and taken was.
—Oh! Beautiful Symmetry of Life!
Such only Heaven could design thus!—
And somehow I knew
that very Sacred Justice
did ride with this horse and me
as with the whole, wide world together!
Forth ever, out of Darkness and into Light
and All this Light Revealeth,
hath and doeth and ever shall!
Praise God! I say. Praise God! Forever and ever!

For and in loving memory of my dear father Robert Carpenter Downer (born 10/27/1910), passed on afternoon of solstice December 21st, 2000, at 90 years of age in Manor Care, Reno, Nevada, USA. Conceived in higher communion while on a speed launch traversing the beautiful turquoise Carribean waters between Belize City and Caye (Key) Caulker Isle in the late afternoon and evening of the 23rd of December, 2000, right after having learned of Robert's transition and as evening stars did "dawn."

OH! GREAT MARINER

Oh! Great mariner,
my father of this life,
        now, you are embarked
upon that vast
        and unknown Sea
wherein and upon
        your own true,
Bright Destiny
        does most surely lie!

Oh! May many a bright
and lofty star
        guide you upon your
own true and special way,
        shining to you
both from without
        and from within arising,
from the Heavenly Kingdom
        we all do share.

My dear father of this life,
now embarked upon
        that Great,
Undying Journey forth
        unto Life and Light,
how many memories
        now flood my heart
of all the kindnesses
        you've shared
over all your 90 years
        just passed;
Godspeed!
        Forever will I
remember you,
        Robert, to others, "bright example"
of wisdom, courage and hope,
        and a special, noble love
all your own
        —and which like a bright light shone!—
and which along with that
        of our most faithful, true,
and loving wife and mother
        —Alice dear—
have given this my life
   such crucial support,
concerning just why I'm here.

Brave mariner,
now again embarked
          upon that vaster
Sea of Truth,
          my love – our love –
be with you
          forever!
And surely our paths
          again shall meet
and ever shall parallel run,
          united in many subtle,
or concrete ways,
          just as they
in this (as all) past life
          have been,
according to God's
          own true,
Great and Perfect Plan,
          and which, most truly,
is our very own.
          Praise God! I say, Praise God!
Amen. Amen.

DURHAM FOG (1994)

I walked out of the fog
one misty day in England,
    in the county, in the city Durham,
at the edge of Cuthbert's tomb,
    and the Magnificent Cathedral
that his bones enshrine
       —this most remarkable man!
I walked out of the fog, I say, and into life,
    this specially charmed *English* life,
but for a little while
    to show the world
all is not lost and that
    there are still wonders about
the likes of which
    the world has yet to see,
still promises to keep,
    so great that those in the past
to them but candles hold!
    Praise God! I say, Praise God!

WINDOW UNTO WALES (SPRING 1995)

Beautiful how it is
when seeing ourselves as we were,
we recall fond memories
and even hard lessons learned,
as in those rich-cultured mining towns
of Wales in bygone times,
I do recall a life
'mid mirth and sorrow,
'mid Heavenly songs
and beautiful singing mountains
and a place of belonging,
and a people to which to belong,
as, now, through some
magical and mysterious means,
this reminiscence great comfort brings!

SPANISH POEM: EL VIAJERO SOLTERO (12/13/96)

Yo digo
que yo he sido
un viajero soltero
en esta vida,
pero por éso le cuento
que he notado un mundo vivo
de cosas, de individuos, de procesos,
de toda clase de cultura
y comportamiento
de nuestra raza humana
y de otras razas:
plantas y animales
todos una familia
¡Claro! porque todos de Dios
y a Dios volviendo.
¡Claro que si!
¡Alaba a Dios
para Siempre!

THE VAGABOND (8/10/99)

The drifter, the wanderer, the vagabond,
one with little attachment
    for this life and world does come
upon such great wonders in same
    and is the better able
to appreciate them
    precisely because of his loose attachment,
his broader identification
    with and definition of
all this we call "home."

JOY (7/31/99)

Some of mortal
life's greatest joys
come from regaining,
if only for brief flashes,
one's sure and certain
knowledge of past lives
and even of ones
yet to come
and the Wondrous Eternal Horizon
such uplifted vision affords.

THE FORGOTTEN (7/22/99)

My heart goes out
to all the forgotten ones
whose spirit is denied
by the worldly "in crowd,"
to these whom God loves
and provides for, though
the worldly would only use and abuse
these innocent flowers.
They are most fine company, indeed,
chastened and unpretentious,
pure of heart and mind and will,
capable of being true friends.
Praise God! Amen.

THE WOMAN'S CRY (7/20/99)

The woman often cries out
with a certain tone of helpless desperation,
for her lot has been that of the victim
of others in life;
yet, for this very reason,
her cry strikes
all the more terror,
for to very Heaven does rise,
to a power beyond
that of the vulgar, worldly order,
that of kill and be killed,
of physical might makes right, *et cetera,*
for her care lies
in the hands and heart
of very God!

HIGH LEVEL (7/13/99)

There are beings
whose high level
of thought and feeling
and willing makes them
powerful and majestic angels,
even though they be
manifest captives of
an incarnate body,
for in their conscious journey,
they still soar high, fly free,
and in their vast and marvelous
flight of consciousness
such great wonders work,
even in this life and world!
Praise God!

Giant Agave with Xiomara Navas-Carbo, Mindo cloud forest area, northern Ecuador.

THE WIZENED ONE – HE COMES AGAIN!

(A Ballad, 6/19/2004)

This song I sing for ye of old,
the one whose life became
a haunting mem'ry full of grace,
a guiding star of fame!

Who was this old and wizened one
who still is now with me?
Was he this me or someone else,
or might he just be thee?

Confusion here will not prevail,
for clear will be my mind!
I'll search the very depths of Time
to feel, to know – the Truth to find!

The Truth, you know, is something more
than meets the shallow eye
or ear. It's heard and seen *Above.*
For such a prize we need not vie.

For rather such a prize descends
from Heaven upon High!
Like light of sun and stars it shines!
And none this can deny!

It tells me now this wizened one
is them and me and you:
is all of us as one wrapped up,
each equal – be no fool!

For life is long and one with Time,
and we are all with this
consistent as the day is long
—and in this there's great gist!

And God to humble souls bestows
that truth which is Himself,
but prideful worshipers of world
to darkness they are cast!

Yet not forever they'll remain,
for wizened one shall come
ever again to mind, to heart,
and save us from all doom.

And when he comes to grace our lives
he'll fill out as the sun
in youthful splendor, radiance
—then so will we, my son.

THE CONNECTION (8/15/2004)

You are the connection,
oh! my soul,
 between and among
all that you have ever known or been,
 presently experience
or yet in future times
 shall come to realize.
You are this unique
 and indispensable connection,
not only as concerns
 your own true,
consciously resynthesizing self,
 but all your fellow
parallelly evolving selves,
 ever mysteriously linked
beyond mere worldly kin.
 You are the great
transcendent essence,
 the spirit who takes it all in,
yet ever remains *more*
 than all worldly life
taken in and of itself
 and as apart
from all that *greater spiritual dimension,*
 in which both it and we are immersed,
the one who exists
 beyond all this
merely objectified or manifest creation.
 And by means of this keen,
transcendent knowledge,

I am now so blessedly unconfused.
Whereas before betimes
        murky clouds obscured my view,
I can see so clearly now
        the true importance
of each *immortal* individual
        and, as a consequence,
of all of us together,
        according to a *Plan*
that has most truly been
        working itself out,
weaving together all distinct threads,
        over all the ages
and very *eons* of time
        since the very Fall,
a plan whose culmination
        still even now goes on amounting
in a searching out of all missing parts
        and novel aspects —all lacks—
to restore very Complete Perfection!
        So take heart:
be ye of good cheer,
        for neither you nor I nor any one of us
shall desist until we get *there*.
        Praise God! I say, Praise God!
Forever and ever.

THE CONNECTION—SHORTENED VERSION (8/18/ 2004)

You are the connection
among *All*
that you've ever known and been
and so will continue:
unique and indispensable
both to your own
as all related selves,
ever accomplishing
life's age-old pursuit,
even in the here and now,
according to the *Higher Plan*:
all encompassing
and perfect in every detail
according to the time.
So take heart:
be ye of good cheer,
for none of us shall desist
until we get *there*!
Praise God! Forever and ever.

TIME, EVOLUTION, AND WORK

Awesome Sangay Volcano, December 1989, Sangay National Park, Ecuador

TIME – A SHRINE (2/22/2001, QUATERNE FORM)

How strangely beautiful is Time!
And what is "Now" becomes a Shrine
    when it recedes to Past's incline,
for then with awe, regards each kind,

    From Heaven, lessons more refined.
How strangely beautiful is Time!
    And all along Life's varied line
ever new wonders, present, fine,

    Unfold themselves within the Vine,
so magic'ly from Source Sublime!
    How strangely beautiful is Time!
This Realm of POSSIBLE – the MIND,

    That ALL contains – yet's unconfined,
appears from Future's World Divine!
    Just wait! We'll see! It's yours! It's mine!
How strangely beautiful is Time!

WORK OF THE SOUL (3/24/2002)

      I hail the great work of the soul,
even as the soul itself!
      Surely it shall not perish,
neither the work nor the essence,
      for the work is
each individual's experience
      throughout all Time,
and each soul is
      the very Spark Divine!

SEVEN POEMS ON *THE SPIRITUAL EVOLUTION* (MY BIRTHDAY: 9/21/2003)

I.

     Life's Story:
Past, Present & Future
     (each moment each one of these)
and Time's all-embracing-ness
     and Spirit's transcendence there-over:
this spirit – this essence – within, beyond the world,
     inspired to Process taking worldly Shape
over time!
     Inward Process: Cause;
Outward Expression: Manifest Effect:
     SPIRITUAL EVOLUTION,
as back from the Fall
     we each and all do rise
in all forms and relations,
     places and times,
each one in Spirit,
     ever unto Thee, Dear Lord!
Ever both with and forth, yet back, to Thee!
     Praise God!

II.

     In youth I was most wont to ponder
the Spiritual Evolution.
     I sang these words,
and with this concept
     the universe encurled,
the universe taken from
     Essential Cause,
that which in each and every

      individual, consciously evolving,
spirit lives!
      Truly so it does
—and unto the Very Highest of ends
      it goes! Praise God!

III.
      Mind-boggling, diverse forms of living creatures
fantastically entrained in this vast process
      called *Living*
have fascinated me for years,
      for lifetimes!
Multiple variations upon many contrasting themes,
      all of which are
perfectly interwoven over time.
      Surely there's something here
more than merely meets
      the external eye or ear, *et cetera*,
some magical, conscious
      essence at work
—oh! God-like essence—
      returning over all the ages
unto the realization of its *perfect self*,
      the which we are all together in.
—Oh! Wondrous *spiritual evolution*!

      Overlapping universal presences,
each uniquely indispensable
      both to every other as well
as to the whole.
      Some *thing* more than
any mere physical process or thing,
      and more than
the mere sum of its parts,
      for transcendent when complete!

Great eternal presences,
        externally expressed betimes
(our many incarnate lifetimes),
        yet ever in transcendent Spirit abiding,
and whose higher knowledge
        spawns these virtues three:
Faith, Hope and Charity
        in each and every one of us.

... So take care as upon your blossoming way you wend
        —oh! my soul! whoever you are –
to smell the roses, to discern the forms,
        for there is such *soul-stirring meaning* here!
This live-saving meaning that lives within,
        yet beyond the confines of any world!
Truly so there is. So onward listen and look
        and in all possible ways perceive and conceive!
Praise God!

IV.
        As a lad I was wont
to fascinate upon diversity and multiplicity in life:
        slimy, creepy toads and newts,
sleek fish, Heavenly birds, wild horses,
        mysterious tapirs and such lovely,
graciously beneficent plants
        when viewed in upshot:
all mutualistically life-sustaining!

        Life's vast display then led me
upon many a wild and free conjecture,
        and soon during university days
had me pouring over
        intimately detailed and ruminated
tomes of varied themes.

From many aspects then I came
to consider this we call *life*:
        the physiological, the anatomical,
the evolutionary, the ecological.
        But *lacking* I found so much of science's
and, so, modern humanity's
        approach to such,
for treating Life as mere *Object*.
        For the most striking of all *Qualities*
– including that much overplayed one called *Quantity* –
        was and is and ever shall remain:
the inner consciousness –yea!– the **Being,**
        in whose perfect and whole grasp
freedom from physical fixation
        is to be attained at last!

And this then ushered in
        a whole higher echelon
of thought and corresponding feeling,
        and the uncovering of *principles*
so wondrous that to do them justice
        I had to sing,
inspired by this God-like super-nature:
        the Being!,
the which in all life forms is expressed
        according to the stage, the time,
the transient state of consciousness,
        and that like an arrow
flyeth unto Truth,
        that somehow and by such lofty laws
is ever blended,
        both now and in all time Past,
Present, and Future – there,
        and yet also here – to the *Goal*:
the very *Omega self-same Alpha*

to which we all aspire,
each indispensably
      complemental to each and every other,
restoring that Perfection
      in which our very Salvation lies.
Oh! Blessed Goal!
      Ever by Grace and to the Glory On High,
and because of God's love for each soul,
      and each soul's love for God,
each in its own special way,
      yet, all as interrelated
together shall attain.
      Truly so we shall.
Praise God! Amen. Amen.

V.
      In my youth
I spoke of *The Spiritual Evolution*
      by whose lofty concept
I sought to embrace
      the spirits in all living forms expressed
and their *Process of Becoming.*
      Embodied in integrated form and function:
whether decomposer, animal, plant, *et cetera,*
      here I beheld the great, self-same *Spirit,*
however diversely manifest,
      for just as it is with *Space,*
and even so as it is with *Time,*
      the Spirit one dimension is,
each aspect of which
      then becomes in our conception
inextricable from the whole;
      and we're each the re-synthesizers of this *All;*
and Spirit's the greatest dimension of this *All!*
      And our awakening unto our own true selves, or self

—why!—'t is concomitant with this
		very rediscovery of God!

VI.
		Spiritual Evolution:
herein
		a concept so very elevating,
enobling.
		The spirit's *at cause*
over all manifest forms and situations,
		the which express their ever further
self-transcending, transmuting conditions,
		as we consciously journey forth,
both individually,
		yet ever inextricably as a collective,
back from the Fall,
		I say, *Back* yet at the same time *Forth*,
out of Darkness and unto Light
		and all the Truth this Light reveals,
this Truth Sublime of God!
		Oh! Such vast symphony to conceive!
Oh! Such vast *Plan* to experience, to live!

VII.
		We find ourselves
reflected in the *deep*
		dark brooding
pool of past existence,
		for mysteriously we are present
throughout the whole of it.
		And if we will only recall,
such beautiful lessons,
		insights, abilities,
therefrom can yet arise,

and unto *brilliant heights,*
unprecedented since the *Fall,*
    ever more superior lessons
that enable us to carry forth
    unto a most gloriously
Whole and Perfect,
    Sky-encompassed Future,
for the Sky's the Limit,
    and there is no limitation here.
Praise God! I say, Praise God!
    Forever and ever!

IN REPETITION (9/3/99)

In repetition over Time,
as experienced, as *lived*,
is keen emphasis given
according to the theme
– and Heavenly lesson –
of the time.
Truly so it is.
Praise God! Amen. Amen.

LIVING PROOF (9/2/99)

Nothing is wrong with me
that the Lord can't fix!
Nothing is wrong with the world
that the Lord can't fix!
And very Time is living proof of this,
for Time lives
and as we experience
the *stream of consciousness*
so we do realize ourselves to be
the very life of very Time!
Praise God! Amen. Amen

FORTH! (9/1/99)

  Knowing great depth of sadness,
one prepares oneself
  for great height of joy,
for life operates this way,
  like a magnificent wheel turning,
each point on which
  is sometimes down and sometimes up,
sometimes forward and sometimes backward,
  yet, ever balanced by
all the other points
  to which it is indispensably connected.

Now, each point is
  an individual spirit's condition,
and as such:
  of indispensable relation
to the whole entire wheel
  ... engine ... train, *et cetera.*
And whether relatively
  up or down,
backward or forward,
  left or right,
the great Wheel of Life
  ever revolveth on,
and with it we each
  and all move forth.
Forth! I say–
  out of Darkness
and unto Light!
  Back –***Back!*** I say–
from the Fall
  and unto God!

HORIZONS IN TIME (10/24/99)

Expand your horizons in Time,
Oh! My soul!
Take heart!
For you have
such great wonders
realized in the Past,
and you will
such great wonders
in the Future
likewise come to realize.
Praise God!

WHERE? (9/1/99)

Where do you put your heart?
What do you value?
Is this merely the worldly
manifest *status quo*?
Or do you recognize
qualities that live within
your heart and mind and will,
but which are not
as yet manifestly fulfilled?
If so, then you
will be brave and strong.
If so, you will find
the where-with-all
to keep moving on,
ever on- and up-ward unto God,
for your sustainer will be that
as yet unachieved goal
whose realization lives in future times
... and lives within your heart and mind
–ever by grace and to the **Glory Divine!**

COALESCENCE (9/1/99)

Strange it is
how in my recollection of places,
so seemingly remote from one another,
and of the distinctive feelings and ethoses
I have sensed there,
as in all the Godly faces and forms,
telling of the abiding spirit and all
its diverse conscious states
and distinctive roles,
there is a coalescence,
a fitting of the pieces together
within my own consciousness,
whose upshot is such
delightful recognition
of Truth and God.
For I see this dawning
as one that has been proceeding
over all the whole ages of Time,
and myself –as any individual self–
an indispensable and immortal thread,
a stream of consciousness
specially weaving this
great continuum together
within my own individual
spiritual enlightenment.
And, somehow, in this we
are all together and related,
made realizedly one
ever by Grace and to the Glory Divine!

DISCOVER WITHIN (8/10/99)

Discover the meanings that exist within
your very own heart and mind and will,
for these are real
and all the world
– or world of worlds –
of mere externalities
are mere epiphenomena
compared with these
great and living ideals,
that whether dormant or awakened to
still within you live!

Therefore, I say,
tap them to greatest overall advantage
as you wind and sing
your way through time,
ever by grace
and to the Glory Divine!

THE WHEEL OF LIFE (8/8/99)

Once you have done
your Heavenly inspired work
in this life and world
then you deserve
to rest and recreate
that in this episode of freedom
you may receive
still higher inspiration from Heaven,
then be about its
work-related fulfilling,
for so life goes on
like a wheel that
rotating moveth forth.
Now each point on the wheel
is sometimes up and sometimes down,
sometimes spinning forward
and sometimes spinning backward.
Yet ever the whole wheel
itself moveth forth!
—upon its very point of contact
pusheth forth!
Aye! For such is life,
and experience, indeed!
And for this I do praise God!

MYSTERIOUS SHIFT (10/3/2003)

How mysteriously shift
our worldly identities and attachments
according to higher governing,
metaphysical laws!
And how beautiful are the patterns
as each soul is elevated in consciousness
so as to perceive them.
How beautiful then
these vast soul histories
and the spiritual lessons
they do teach,
ever onward and upward leading
and in ubiquitously interrelated fashion!
Truly so it is.
Praise God! And Hallelujah! shout.

POSIT (8/5/2003)

      Posit this:
that all the soul's great
      and vast realm
of sequential experience
      unifies in Divine Truth,
whose glorification,
      whose proof *first within,*
constitutes its very purpose
      and most sublime end.
Praise God! Amen. Amen.

AWARE (7/31/99)

Those aware of the eternal life
find patience with the present
one they're living,
knowing it to be a stage
in the immortal progression,
and that all mortality
taken in and by itself
but a delusion is;
and that on sacred Time's vast horizon,
in all conscious evolving,
life unto Perfection
awakens again,
Praise God! Amen.

INTERIOR WORK (7/22/99)

Do not disparage
the interior work
that each individual soul makes
and which often
is made seemingly alone,
for this is life's
very greatest work
in obligate partnership
with all others,
for foremostly
with God!

Misty cascade, midday, lower Baños-Puyo route, Pastaza Province, Ecuador

TRACINGS (8/99)

Conception is described
in images resulting from tracings
of the soul's motion,
its activity through Time.
And to take the time
to appreciate this great wonder
is to enter into the *Seventh Day*
assigned by God for Paradise!

TRAVELING (7/18/99)

See traveling as energy exchanges
and, what's more,
as consciousness exchanges:
dynamic, evolving interactions,
for all life is a journey,
even for those
who seem mere armchair travelers
yet who in spirit can
venture very far, indeed!
Truly so they can.
Praise God! Amen. Amen.

ANY MOMENT (7/14/99)

Do not overlook any moment of time,
including the present, for its unique
yet interrelated importance;
rather rejoice in each new,
as each old, moment,
looking forward in faith
toward the completion,
the resolution, of all Time
—yea!– in very Perfection Divine!

NO LOOSE THREAD (7/14/99)

This concerning life:
that no loose thread
in all our ever-begun relations
in Time
shall forever unconnected remain!
And, for this reason,
such great faith have I
as forth together
with all fellow spirits
in this we call "life"
I go. Praise God!

WORDS, LANGUAGE, BOOKS, LIBRARIES

DOWN LONG LIBRARY AISLES (1997?)

Sometimes looking down long library aisles
I see you there,
    the soul of my soul,
reading and writing
    —Oh!—so contentedly,
working some mighty works
    in some unique and precious
Heavenly land of the blessed!
    And, perceiving you there,
I know *all is well*
    in this *land of souls*,
and that there too somewhere,
    some time, I shall find
my own special abode
    —abode of the soul, abode of hope!
Surely so. Praise God!

A LIBRARY MOST ENTERTAINING! (1997?)

Imagine, if you can,
a library where books took on
very lives and consciousness
and wills of their own,
each conversing with the other
according to its own
distinctive content and values,
some in sympathy, harmoniously complementing,
others in antipathy, themselves combating.
Aye! 't would be a library most entertaining,
for, in fact, each living being
is like a given book,
and the present life one lives
is one episode in such,
yet all together are written within
God's holy Book of Life
—that which immortal is,
unborn and undying is!
Surely so! Praise God!

THE LIVING BOOK (1997)

Imagine, if you can, a *living book*,
and your ever reading and writing it!
A *living book*, I say,
one that feels and talks back,
is struck and bleeds, and, in turn,
strikes and makes bleed,
for you are this *living book*
and so is each and every one you meet!
Surely it is so. Praise God!

BOOK OF LIFE (INSPIRED POEM WHILE BATHING) (12/12/96)

Let the pages
of God's holy Book of Life
freely turnéd be,
for unimpeded:
those blessed thoughts
each succeeding which
is the logical conclusion
of all those that have gone
before,
since the very Fall,
that restored
in Truth Divine,
as One in Spirit,
we may all be,
like bubbles rising
to the surface
of Heavenly Reality,
there, at last, to be free!

THOUGHTS ON WORDS (2/27 & 3/8 & 3/12 2001)

Words are strange.
They each have a certain
    unique history of spiritually
experienced meaning
    associated with them.
They are vibration,
    each a unique combination of sounds
corresponding to inner states
    of consciousness
—spiritual states these!
    And herein lies their mystery.
Praise God!

Yet merely manifest words can be misleading,
    as can any overt,
externalized expression.
    And for this reason,
it is better to strive
    for spiritual understanding,
for this is to arrive
    at the root cause
and true grasp
    of all that goes forth in Life.
Truly so it is. Praise God!

Words, as all manifest works and noticings,
are nothing
    without the Heavenly inspiration
that compels them,
    whatever the spiritual plane
one dwells upon.
    Praise God! Amen. Amen.

There is magic in words
when spoken/written
        with true and inspired meaning,
imbued in the very medium
        through which they
transmitted are. Praise God!

        Think and write and speak words
that uplift and expand
        the conceptions
of those around you,
        rather than these
limit or reduce.

        Words attempt to communicate
the individual soul's progression
        in all its dimensions
and would fall short
        in this audacious endeavor
were it not
        for the miracle of suggestion.
Praise God! Amen. Amen.

WORDS (2/23/2001)

Words are like
psychic smoke signals
into which spirits impute
as vastly various meanings
as there are individuals
and times in which
to place them.
Praise God! Amen. Amen.

WORDS (3/6/2001)

Words often reflect attitudes.
They are subtle things
        that contain long histories
in their formation.
        Learn to be free with them
and creative, that more
        of the whole and perfect truth
may come out of you
        by their means,
both as yourself
        and all others concerns.
Learn to be wondrously
        honest by means of words!
Praise God! Amen. Amen.

        There is something
intensely spiritual about reading
        and writing – an act of faith!,
a labor of love!—
        for a give
and take communion
        transpires within
the higher spiritual dimension;
        and, thereby, whole worlds are moved
as the soul blossoms
        unto greater wholeness and perfection.
And, as a consequence,
        all the manifest world
of Creation is transformed
        from the subtle plane
within us all. Praise God!

Pay attention to the feelings
that the sounds of words
        arouse in you.
Unite instinct with logic,
        for thereby
you will find the key
        to both words' ideal meanings
and their evolutionary history,
        by means of varying associations,
according to the individual beings,
        through Time – and how these all
relate to our shared, our mutual discovery
        of the great and universal Truth,
through all our vast
        and diversely contrasting experiences!

SPEECH (3/11/2001)

Speech and its super-terranean
forms called writing, poetry and song,
I realize derive from breathing,
from that great eternal rhythm,
which like the heartbeat,
which like the ebb and flow,
of the ocean's tides,
and all similar cycles,
carries us both on and through,
like some great revolving wheel,
that moves us forth.

Now, just consider this:
wherever it is
upon this mighty
universal wheel you sit,
your very life,
your moving forth,
depends upon the WHOLE OF IT,
whatever "up" or "down" position
you seem to be on its revolving,
for ever the rolling wheel
advanceth forth!
Praise God!

"POETRY" (7/11/95)

Poetry is the mystic way
spirits have of communicating with one another.
So is music, so is dreaming,
and so are many other "things" we name,
in ultimate analysis all the same.
Surely it is so
—and wondrous to experience, to live!
Praise God!

PAUSES (12/13/96)

In
Silence
we are
taught so much,
as in the pauses
between the poetic verses
we receive
that higher meaning
from "Upstairs",
from the Source.
Surely so!
Of course!

THE REALITY OF LANGUAGE (3/11/2001)

The reality of language,
music and song
is a subtle one.
Its capacity
first to inwardly realize
and then to outwardly express
TRUTH
is also inseparable
from this TRUTH.
It is the great synthesis,
the magnificent summation,
the holy work of the soul,
each and every
who is the realization of such,
over ALL OF TIME,
that is our great story,
our becoming,
as ever forth
out of Darkness and into the Light
we do proceed,
back from the Fall and unto God!

THOUGHTS UPON READING "MOSSES ..." (5/24/2003)

... Long Time Ago,
      or so it seems,
      Nathaniel Hawthorne penned
      "Mosses From an Old Manse",
      intent on communicating
      his impressions, his insights, his wisdom,
      then and to future climes.
      – Puritanical and pure his vision was
      and still remains!

... And Now
      from this quaint and ornate
      and long-inviting tome,
      I sit me down to read
      these yellowed pages
      in whose very patina of Time
      I pick up an essence ...

... Something So Subtle
      I must read between the lines,
      allowing the words chosen
      and the whole timing and circumstance
      that led to my now reading them
      to act as springboards for the Imagination ...

... Each Imagination Unique,
      Hawthorne's and mine
      and any other's so inclined,
      yet undeniably interconnected
      – and, too, by grace of
      specially imbued and
      living symbols –
      as in our very waking

and dream worlds
we do meet
in this vast sweep
of past and present
and future times ...

For That of the Very Essence
of communication's blessed
intent does carry on
to meet its mark,
however near or far away
in Time's report
– and like a very
miracle to realize ...

... And So
it is like "mosses from an old manse"
that we upon each other grow.
And even our mortal remains,
including these penned words
– and our very bones –
strangely come to remind ourselves
of the Mutual Company
we do ever keep
and that
no manifest thing,
however tiny or colossal,
celebrated or obscure,
is without
its higher Cause,
its higher, all-connecting
Significance!

– Praise God! I say, Praise God!
And Hallelujah! shout.

LANGUAGE (7/27/99)

Those who are onto
the spirit of any given language
grasp the sheer and universal importance of
this particular vibration and its intrinsic link
to all diverse, yet interrelated,
spiritual states and conditions.
This then allows the realization
of genial art both in
the expression, or giving,
as in the reception of communication.
And by *vibration* I mean
sound, sight, smell, taste,
feel, kinesthesia, *et cetera*,
– and all of these
most surely related are.

WRITING (7/27/99)

Writing involves faith,
a subtle plane of communication
that all the very ages spans,
that operates on the principle
that every sincere and heartfelt will
to communicate is registered
to all those receptive souls
– and give and take with this's involved.
Truly so. Praise God!

READING AND WRITING (7/22/99)

Reading and writing can provide
a sort of greatly accelerated
consideration of one's own
and others' experience of life,
allowing one to more directly
survey the spiritual panorama
in time, the better to learn
those great Heavenly lessons
God therein and there-through teaches.

A BOOK (7/18/2003)

There is a great
sense of satisfaction that comes
    with writing a book
with one's thoughts
    well verbally expressed
and beautifully illustrated
    with images or music.
The book puts *it all together*
    to share with all others,
like presenting one's testimony,
    one's case before Heaven.
Surely there must be
    a very high Heavenly ideal
corresponding to what we mortals
    shape and fashion into books
– howsoever we do betimes
    miserably fail at this.
So may the dear Lord God
    inspire us each to write
his/her own unique and special book
    – one absolutely indispensable
to the whole of universal becoming!
    Praise God! Amen. Amen.

THE GENIUS OF WORDS (7/18/99)

The genius of words
and word combinations
is to be appreciated by
the one who understands
their root origins within
the depths and heights and vast expanses
of spiritual history,
and the Heavenly Ideals
to which these lead
in our ongoing
discovery of most holy Truth.
Praise God!

WRITING (7/16/99)

Writing is more than
the mechanical act thereof;
its product: more than
dried ink on paper!
Similarly, life as experienced,
as lived, more than its
mere physical record is!
As with all things
and aspects of creation,
it is the individual soul
who preserves all,
who synthesizes all,
who resolves all:
in Space and all things therein,
in Time and all moments therein,
for *in Spirit*.
And it is in the all preserving Spirit that
we are most surely one,
ever by grace and to the Glory Divine!

VALUE OF A WORD (7/12/99)

The feeling of a word
spoken in a poem
or sung in a song
is not to be measured
by physical means alone,
but in sublime manner,
as all pure spirits know,
as tests the heart and mind and will,
according to standards
purely spiritual, as spirits
to spirits call,
each according to
its own special role
throughout all the universe.
Praise God!

A VOICE ... A WORD (9/23/2004)

A voice is more
than strikes the ear,
vibrations carried through the air
–for *who* originated this call?!

A word in printed form
is more than image upon
the retina conveyed to brain
–for from *within* it came!

Each particle in energetic process involved,
too, is a voice, a word
whose meaning is its cause
–for this within me lives! Praise God!

CONCERNING MUSIC AND BEAUTY

MELODIES: A HYMN TO CREATION (AN EVER SO FREE VERSE POEM) (9/1/2002)

The melodies that come to me
are such Heavenly life-giving streams,
        descending to this dark world of woe
like rays of the sun,
        they brighten every day
– give hope!

        – Oh! that I could do justice right here on Earth
to these sweet, refinéd airs
        by very Heaven upon my heart
strings played, so pure, in tune, on time,
        extolling their uplifting messages
both in and through all mediums,
        then grasped, agreed, and manifest perceiving
these in others made – for shared
        –Aye!– 't would the fulfillment be
of so many lost hopes and dreams,
        within all the Fullness of Time,
within all these intricate constructions
        –Oh! wondrously diverse and interwoven songs!–
from out the very far reaches
        of mysterious *Space*, and –what's more– of *Time*
and *Spirit* all-transcending.

For Hope's Music does brighten *every* day
in such universal relatings, processings,
        from such Glorious Dispensations!
And –Oh!– how clear this rings
        in *Our* Most Magnificent Choir Divine!

So sing on! I say, Sing on
        –Yea!–   until the very last possible note is sung!
Praise God! Amen. Amen.

THE PIANIST (3/11/2001)

       One knows comfort
and ease in life's flow
       when, as a pianist,
rightly premeditating
       his musical course
of performance,
       one plays on blissfully,
borne ahead by a
       greater grasp of all
Time and Becoming!

MUSIC (3/7/2001)

Music describes
different states of animation,
        different times. And
as these contrast and interrelate
        and find and celebrate
that common thread,
        so the music grows
more great! For this common thread
        is the individual soul itself,
consciously uniting all times, all notes,
        and even all fellow souls!
Praise God!

BEAUTY (7/30/99)

Beauty is
discerning enlightened presences
and the noble principle
that reflects itself
in all kinds
of all uniting
correspondence, or parallels.
Truly so Beauty is. Praise God!

TRANSPOSE (7/19/99)

Learn to transpose
between the visual and the acoustical,
     as in the sight reading of music
and in other ways to link
     the input of diverse senses
to achieve brilliant
     and concerted conceptions
and, when appropriate,
     their willed expressions
upon this or any plane.
     Praise God! Amen. Amen.

BEAUTIFUL (7/18/99)

How beautiful is life,
even this current one we live,
when seen from the
Eternal Perspective!
For Beautiful is God.

A MUSICAL BALM (8/99)

I like that music
which sings in the breeze
 and chirps forth from the crickets,
which the birds in the sky do sing
 and the worms and snakes do hum
and which needs no human
 agency to be known,
for it is pure balm to my soul.
 Praise God!

Alice Marie Gottschalk Downer, a beautiful pianist and mother of author, hiking the Rubicon Trail, W. Lake Tahoe, California

ECSTASY

(a sonnet, conceived and dedicated to my mother Alice Marie Gottschalk Downer, a beautiful pianist, on her 91st birthday, March 2, 2004)

The crashing sound of thunder round me rolls,
as lightning spears the ground from Heav'n on High,
and glor'ous music heart and mind now fills,
compelling me to lend in song my cry.

Unique's the melody so pure I sound.
'T is born of all before I've lived and known.
Yet, too, in it is Future where I'm bound
–a call supreme I seek just as a crown.

Oh! Lord! May I as worthy so be judged,
unleashed of heart, of mind, of will, of voice,
attuned to universe and not begrudged
the *ecstasy* so wild and free—my choice!

For like the lightning's clap would I now be,
to soar o'er **all** in perfect **harmony**!

INTELLIGENCE, WISDOM, GENIUS, AND INSPIRATION

LISTEN

(2/27/2001, after "hearing" a melody upon awakening from my dream)

       Listen, oh! my soul,
and you will hear
       life's wondrous song
unfolding uniquely, as never before.
       Truly so you will.
Praise God! I say, Praise God!

REMEMBERING (7/11/95)

      Remembering ... remembering,
I am brought home
    to wherever home has been
or will yet be!
      ... And this is such a sweet truth
that within me sings.
      Surely so. Praise God! Amen.

INSPIRATION (3/13/2001)

A brilliant insight
is to be valued
    above all worldly measure!
It is Heaven's gift!
    And do not try
to confine it
    by worldly means.
It is a beautiful poem,
    a piece of music or a song,
the appreciation of some fine
    and revealing landscape,
a painting wrought
    by God with His brush
of Time. To appreciate this
    sublime meaning in life
is True Value, True Possession,
    not worldly contrived and bogus.
Praise God!   I say, Praise God!

THOUGHTS ON GENIUS (3/10/2001)

1)   The secret of genius is:
weaning oneself from worldly infatuation
        that one may perceive clearly,
conceive rightly,
        no longer be subjugated
to worldly delusion, a.k.a.. sin.
        Truly it is so. Praise God! Amen.

2)   As one liberates
one's mind and heart and will
        from worldly tyrannies, so,
one comes to cultivate
        one's own true genius,
and thereby
        one's life is saved
—ever by Grace and to the glory of God!

3)   Half the battle
of success in life, I find,
        is not heeding
one's ill-motivated detractors,
        who are only thinking
of their own isolated advantage
        —and I hasten to add,
one's not so becoming
        when it to others comes!

4)   Finding that
in one's own life which is uplifting
        with which to identify
and this to make live
        surely such great blessing is!

5)   Overcoming worldly attachments,
one rises to Heavenly heights,
        to sublime levels
one in consciousness ascends,
        thus, to win out over sin,
ever by grace and to the glory
        of God. Praise God! Amen.

6)   How I love honesty, spontaneity,
and the right and power
        of each unique individual soul
to its *own self be true*.
        Surely so I do.
Praise God! And Hallelujah! shout.

7)   Because God cares,
He inspires each one of us
        to play our own special role
toward all others,
        to save the holy possibility
for all life on Earth!
        Praise God!

UNLOCKED TREASURE (3/13/2001)

So much can be unlocked
in the world about you
by gaining insight into
the psychology of those about you,
brilliantly inspired visualization
through revealed visions
of all these unique,
yet interrelated, soul histories,
and how your own therewith
is woven into
a sublimeTapestry
whose perfecting
lies yet ahead
upon Future's glowing horizon!

... There is a sense
of inner perfecting,
of restoring all
that was lost,
that is realized
by the introspective soul
and wherefrom all true,
great treasures flow.
Praise God! Hallelujah!

THE FURTHER QUESTION: THE ESSENE REAWAKENS—AN ANTIPOPHORA (3/21/2002)

Is there a value in
questioning that as yet unquestioned,
    in asking that ever more subtle question
for each and for every given
    situation/relation, though vulgar society,
for this yet finer query
    does pounce upon one?!

    – Yes, brave soul, 't is surely so,
for one's very life upon this higher attunement,
    this with-world-discontented wit,
depends, for when
    our inner promptings we ignore,
life's very greater quest/train of reason
    we do, in fact, deny and thereby self-betray!
Oh! then (dark day!),
    our true zeal, our fine zest
–Aghast!– is lost!
    Perversely our minds, our hearts,
from Higher Source are disconnected.
    We have chosen Hell, that in effect is:
state of dis-virtue; dark, woeful condition
    –and all for fault of questioning,
and to worldly *status quo*
    –such lie!– ourselves subjecting.
And all that is Perfect and Whole
    –Oh!– sublime Truth forgetting
that truth which though from without prompted
    ever from within must be awakened ...

Therefore –Oh! Lord!– for this I pray:
　　　open up the Bright Gates
of yearning query in me –in all!–
　　　that may not be lost, but found
My Very Soul,
　　　in this my present life,
as in all parallel lives,
　　　for we all *One In Spirit* are!
Truly so. Praise God! Praise God!

SELF-KNOWLEDGE: AN INSPIRED THOUGHT (12/12/96)

Hath not the spirit
knowledge of itself,
who when freed from
worldly delusion
by Heavenly Supernature
riseth unto Truth?!
Surely so it hath. Praise God!

DELIVERANCE! (6/19/2000)

How do I deliver myself from a whole mess
of materialistic claims and limitations?!
I simply ask a preciously inspired, further question,
one that no materialistic philosophy
can ever explain away.
Such as *What is consciousness?,*
What is spirit?,
Who am I?
and, by the same token,
Who are we?
What unites the external world
with the inner spirit of each one of us?,
et cetera, et cetera.
For these are life's
great undeniable questions;
and these so called "unanswerable questions"
ever put all materialistic philosophies to shame!
Praise God! Amen. Amen.

IMAGINATION (9/1/99)

      The intelligence of imagination
allows both
      remembrance of past realizations
and the prescience of future ones.
      This is because
one thereby taps the universal mind
      in which the vastly great
Realm of the All Possible,
      not only exists, *but lives!*
And we move forth within it,
      but even more to the point,
it moves forth
      unto all hallowed perfection
in us! Praise God!

IMAGINATION (8/4/99)

       For those who
walk alone in life,
       the Imagination becomes
a brilliant window
       affording many a precious insight
and higher communion
       even when
not a word is spoken,
       or not a soul
seems to be around.
       Truly so it does.
Praise God! Amen.

HIGH PERSPECTIVE (8/2/99)

Intelligence waxes
as worldly pride wanes,
    since the conscious
is freed to ascend
    to higher perspectives,
in *Space* – and what's more –
    in *Time*, for most of all
in *Spirit!* Truly so it does.
    Praise God!

ENLIGHTENMENT (7/27/99)

What hath any one
more than his soul?
Surely nothing worldly
even begins to compare,
for in his soul
is the true possession of all
things and so much more
than things, or objects!
This possession is called:
Spiritually Enlightened Consciousness
– all in relationship to God!
Praise God!
And Hallelujah! shout.

GENIUS (7/27/99)

Genius, true insight,
is hatched from
the very immensity
of all Time
and Spiritual Evolution!
Praise God! Amen.

IMAGINATION (7/27/99)

Tapping higher planes
of consciousness requires one
to make sacrifice of
petty, worldly confining attachments.
Imagination enters here,
for it liberates the awareness
from the imperfect
and the unwhole.
Praise God! And Hallelujah! shout.

TO REVIVE (10/16/2003)

       To revive the essence of past times
in one's heart and will and mind
       is to re-weave precious threads,
indispensable to the glorious tapestry
       of all Creation,
ever by grace and to
       the exceeding glory of God! Amen.

GESTATION (A MINUTE POEM) (2/1/2005)

I sit alone to know my thoughts
– of these there's lots!
Reflections rule.
No need of school.
It's here within my mind and heart!
– Now, *where to start?*,
how to express?,
makes for duress,
until I know that great "here's how!"
in here and now
to make dreams live
that I may give!

DREAMS, DESIRES, PROPHECIES, ET CETERA

DREAMS – A POEM (2/25/2001)

       Dreams are amazing
in that what one conceives
       and is imaged, sounded, smelled, tasted, felt, *et cetera, et cetera,*
one is and realizes oneself so to be
       within one's ever universally relating spiritual state.
–And what vast overviews of life,
       spanning many lifetimes,
one can in dreams
       in relatively few nights
attain! Praise God! Amen.

DESIRE (3/14/2001)

Since one is controlled and limited
by what one desires and becomes attached to,
whether realized in this life or not,
take care, oh! my soul,
to choose well
that which you desire.

THE STRANGE (3/13/2001)

It is the strange, the unexpected,
that often frightens one,
even though that or whom
one does not yet know
in certain neglected ways
has attained a better state
than one has as yet known
(since the Fall).
And herein lies the great value
of all such strangeness
becoming familiarly known
again. Praise God! Amen. Amen.

Perito Moreno Glacier from east side, Perito Moreno National Park, Argentina

AFTERMATH OF SUPERSTORM (4/29/2002)

```
                    X
                  X   X
                X   X   X
                   ... Bright stars
              ... Fresh, clean air
                     – Devastation's past!
              ... All is still.
                     ... Mind is sharp
              ... and pure.
   X                 ... Heart also          X
   X          ... Will.                      X
 X   X                 ... Candles being lit   X   X
   X          ... first inside               X
   X                 ... then out.           X
              "We're here!",
                     they sincerely announce,
              "and the soul
                     is not an alien
              in the universe!"
                     Praise God!
                  X   X   X
                    X   X
                      X
```

YEARNINGS – A BRIEF (OCTOBER, 2000, RENO)

Yearnings
calling sweetly
... my angel beckons,

There to
Higher Futures,
to which I now go!

Worldly
values, concerns
– Go! I won't have them!

... Soon now,
I am soaring
over all the world!

Those whom
I once did know,
better I do know now:

Complete,
Relational,
Unified and Whole!

I see
Us all in this
Great Resolution,

OF ALL!
FOREVER IN,
PERFECT GRACE AND LOVE!

A GOLDEN DOOR (7/21/2003)

For those who hope for *More,*
to weep's a Golden Door!
Though their visions
this present life's outstripped,
seen through idealistic tears
and heard through
Heavenly in-misted ears,
this present life's transformed,
linked by Heavenly means
–for which Belief is Key!–
to higher planes
and future times.
Praise God! Amen. Amen.

PRESAGE (9/1/99)

       Such wondrous certainty
presages worldly life's
       momentous positive event,
for the miracle has
       already been
achieved within
       before it's ever
expressed without.
       Truly so it is.
Praise God! And Hallelujah! shout.

Sunset from Mount Chimborazo, Chimborazo Province, Ecuador. 12/99

NIGHT AND DAY (9/14/99)

Subtle is the night
and full of dreams,
dark and mysterious
and full of stars.
But when the morning dawns,
our star, the Sun,
glorifies our world
as a new day
unlike that of
any day before,
and any that shall come after,
ensues with its own

special Heavenly lesson,
one sent express, direct
    from God,
for each and for all
    to learn and then
to teach in turn.
    Truly so is the dawning
and the rising to the zenith
    and the setting of this sun
as the world spins on in
    its revolutions about this sun,
that, in turn, courses its way
    throughout the very universe
as all we spirits resolve our way
    Back from the Fall,
Yea!, to Highest Truth,
    to God!

LIFE IS DREAMED (8/2/99)

Life is dreamed,
not merely a machine
made of sticks and stones,
but experienced, felt,
thought, willed,
by all existing, individual beings,
somehow ever united
within this great spiritual dimension.
Know this, oh! my soul,
and from the worldly lie
go ye free!
Truly so do.
Praise God! And Hallelujah! shout.

DREAMS (7/12/99)

The dream process
is intimately, inextricably,
    involved with
both memory and prophecy,
    as well as actualized present realization.
Pay attention to your dreams,
    for these reveal
life's higher spiritual meaning,
    purpose, origin, end.
Praise God! Amen.

ANGEL OF FROGS (A DORSIMBRA) (10/24/2004)

... Remember Angel fine and pure and good,
who came to me one night in blissful dream.
In glorious aura, multitudes there stood,
of frogs: vast forms – such beauty they did beam!

    Ethereal,
    translucent through,
    the frogs *in love*
    there stood to view.

As I in wonder sought to grasp this scene,
reality of some yet higher plane,
Frogs' Savior then upon me smiled
... Remember Angel fine and pure and good!

ANIMALS, INCLUDING
WILD HORSES

LOON: A TITLED SENRYU (5/18/2002)

**   ****   ******

Loon's haunting love song

Beckons me to realms beyond

Northern lights afar

**   ****   ******

WILD HORSE DESTINY (1/17/2001)

Something there is of ***Destiny***
that calls to me
in the ***wild horse***
who runs so free
upon the remotest
desert and plain,
mountain range
or valley green,
for there is a ***Rightness*** here
and an ***ancestral precedence***
dating back millions of years!
Surely this egotistical upstart
called ***civilized man***
shall not be allowed
to extinguish
either this powerfully beautiful line
of ascent from ancient times,
or that ***by-God-valued Freedom***
without which
the very soul of Horsekind,
would be denied.

... And there is something implicit here too
in the very Destiny of all we call "**the West**"
that affirms: ***"Without wild horses***
free to roam the vast unfenced expanses,
the West itself its very soul would lose!"
May Heaven forbid!
Praise God!

CIMARRON STALLION: A TITLED HAIKU (5/30/2002)

Cimarron stallion

Galloping freedom's idol

Pure spirit you are

"El Espanto"- medicine hat, paint stallion sacred to Indians, together with his band (other band in background). 1980 Southern Pancake Range, eastern Nevada at dusk.

POEM TO WILD HORSES (1995)

I write a poem
about the wild horse,
'cause there's a lot of feeling here,
albeit much long suffering
and abuse by man— most gruesome!
... Yet, too, vast wide-open spaces,
and MANY lives lived out
with Grace and in Joyful Freedom!

–'T is a saga of the Old West
–and I believe the New–
this story of the wild horse,
this enduring, wind-drinking
runner of desert and plain,
as –Alas!– of very Time!

His story is one with yours and mine.
May he reach far upon this Earth Plane!

For 't is a saga of what this Land is yet to be,
of a Destiny yet unfulfilled,

when Man and Horse in Freedom live
once again with mutual Respect.

POEM TO WILD HORSES AS REVISED BY MY FATHER ROBERT CARPENTER DOWNER, 1997

I write a poem
about the wild horse,
    'cause there's a lot of feeling here,
albeit much suffering
    and abuse – most gruesome!
Yet, too, vast wild spaces to share,
    and MANY lives lived out
with Grace and in Freedom!
    –'T is a saga of the Old West
–and I believe the New!
    This story is the wild horse's best,
this enduring, wind-drinking,
    runner of desert and plain,
as –Alas!– of very Time!
    His story is one with yours and mine.
–May he reach far upon this Earth plane!
    For 't is a saga of what this Land is yet to be,
of a *Destiny* yet unfulfilled,
    when Man and Horse *in Freedom live*
once again with *mutual Respect.*

DIVERSE CREATURES (8/7/99)

How I love
the natural world around me,
full of all the Lord's creatures!
To me it is
not the vicious,
material, or physical, machine
that insensitive, externally fixated
scientists often portray it as,
but rather a place
of spiritual perfecting!
And all the diverse
states and conditions
possible in conscious spirit
here find their
outwardly manifest expression,
in form and feature,
face and behavior,
kindred and kind.
And I to each of these
related am. Praise God! Amen.

FREEDOM

POEM TO FREEDOM (1995) (SEQUEL TO "POEM TO WILD HORSES")

      –I like it wild and rough and free,
being in a place and in a company
      where life must prove its mettle true
and there's no sissying pampering,
      for one must become universally attuned
through virtuous and honest striving,
      even as all creatures do
to Life's true cause and meaning
      and, so, to that *Great Beyond*,
recognizing all kinds as *in Spirit ONE!*

      –No fence confining: horse running free!
–No murderous eye denying: eagles soaring to the sun!
      Each individual being,
in whatever house or body dwelling,
      seeking and finding
true Wisdom, true Freedom;
      living, breathing, with mutual,
respect and reverence,
      praising we each in every possible way,
that Divine Nature which reigneth over all!

Cycad back-lit, late afternoon, Royal Hawaiian Botanical Gardens, Big Island, Hawaii, 8/2004.

THE FLAME OF FREEDOM (3/13/2002)

       Candle flame flickers free
with wild will its own,
       shall not by *any*
worldly confines be bound,
       for such would only
put out this wonder,
       whose burning *a special spirit's*
pure, bright shining spells
       –and *lighteth* up all the world!
Praise God!

WILDERNESS (8/30/99)

Notice the importance of wilderness
to the prophets, to the avatars, to the Messiah,
    with their forty days and forty years,
for in this solitude one is freed
    from mundane human pettiness and greed,
from ignoble worldly societies
    with their false values,
cleared of mind
    and purified of heart and will
so as to purely commune with God
    in the harmonizing company
of all diversely formed or unformed,
    but universal kindred spirits.

THE WIND IN OUR SAILS (7/26/99)

Where do we get
the wind in our sails
if not from the Heavens on High?
For merely to live life
without a grasp
of its higher spiritual meaning,
of *where* we've come from
and to *where* we're bound,
is surely no true living,
but only a mere
going through the motions.
Surely none of this
the Light of Day shall stand.
Praise God! Amen. Amen.

POWER (8/18/99)

       With enlightened knowledge
comes the power
       to rise from out
the depths
       to higher heights.
Truly so it does.
       And this is known inside.
Praise God! I say, Praise God!

TO FIT LIFE IN (10/16/2003)

Do not try to fit life
into some narrow repressive box
where it clearly
does not belong,
but rather let
the spirit of life go free
to expand unto
its fullest potentiality,
there to realize
its true wholeness and perfection,
in relation
not just to every thing,
or every place,
or every time,
but most surely
to every fellow one.
– And this, as only it can be,
in God,
in the pure Love of God!

SPONTANEOUS (7/12/99)

Such a great
universally attuned wisdom
I often do recognize
in innate, instinctual,
spontaneous conceptions
and the inspired actions
that from these flow.
Praise God!

BIRD-BORNE BALLAD (1/10/2005)

Hobo-rhymed thoughts
now come to me –
by-bird-whispered melodies!
No money have I, but what I've got
is all the best in life that's free!

Carefree as bird who soars above,
whose home is wind and rain and sun,
I chart my course 'mid star-strewn fun;
and that of life which most I love –
't is Freedom's triumph when this life's done!

REVERENCE FOR LIFE, CONSERVATION OF THE NATURAL WORLD

PEACE ON EARTH, GOOD WILL TO ALL KINDS – A FIALKA (EASTER, 2001 A.D.)

When think I of how we should live on
this Earth, I am stricken with anguish
am singed with remorse, for all the
quite bad deeds stacked up like a curse, like
a million past lessons all failed and
each worse – made by all means perverse! So
up rise I this moment demanding
a change, defying the sluggard,
embracing my kin, in this greater
Dimension of Lion and Lamb ...

Male Mountain Tapir (endangered species, see Andean Tapir Fund webpage: www.andeantapirfund.com) Southern slope Sangay Volcano. 2:40 p.m. 12/24/96.

CHAI! CHAI! CHAI! CHAI! (6/19/99)

     Chai! Chai! Chai! Chai!
Chai! Chai! Chai! Chai!
    in these Andes so high
is how in Quichua,
    Puruhaes stoically cry *Cold!*
And I'm one who's here
    as a foreigner, *extranjero*,
precisely to prick the conscience,
    for noble sentiment's no fool,
to awaken the frozen heart
    even in places quite cool
—and this is also practical, for sure!—

for this *living fossil* tapir
is disappearing from the Earth,
         because *la carne es rica*
and because blind traditions to boot
         devastate its cloud forest
and páramo habitats
         like there's no tomorrow:
cattle cultures and meat eaters who
         egotistically don't give a hoot
that the highland's *living sponge*
         by their gross appetites is being undone,
that the precious and life-sustaining
         soils are sliding down;
and that this ancient seed disperser,
         and master of balance,
this mythical bringer
         of dance and good cheer,
the mountain tapir,
         of ignorance and brute cruelty
made victim is
         –by such dire disregard!–
that as a consequence,
         without this special, animating spirit,
the forests, the soils,
         the gentle, pure breeze,
the clear mountain streams
         –all this Paradise
to oblivion descends
         ... and the Earth's
left with a fatal hole
         in its heart

where once so gracefully
      the mountain tapir was wont,
as in its ozone layer
      to be scorched by the Sun
and frozen by the Moon!
      Chai! Chai! Chai! Chai!
Chai! Chai! Chai! Chai!

THE HUMAN SPECIES AS GREEDY UNTO ITSELF (SUMMER 1992?)

Imagine, if you will,
the human species as greedy unto itself,
as thoughtless of the other species,
as inconsiderate, irreverent, cruel – and worse!
Well, such has our kind become:
not "mankind" but "mancruel",
and perverse: unwilling to perceive
the great wonder there
in all these living creatures
who share Life and this planet Earth as home
and only ask on the part of man
some moderation, some modicum,
of respect of basic right and freedom
to uniquely live and be,
that they in freedom can complete,
can do their part
to make the world a perfect whole.
–Oh! God! Surely some blessed day
and Golden Age of Righteousness *they*
–and *we* most surely will!

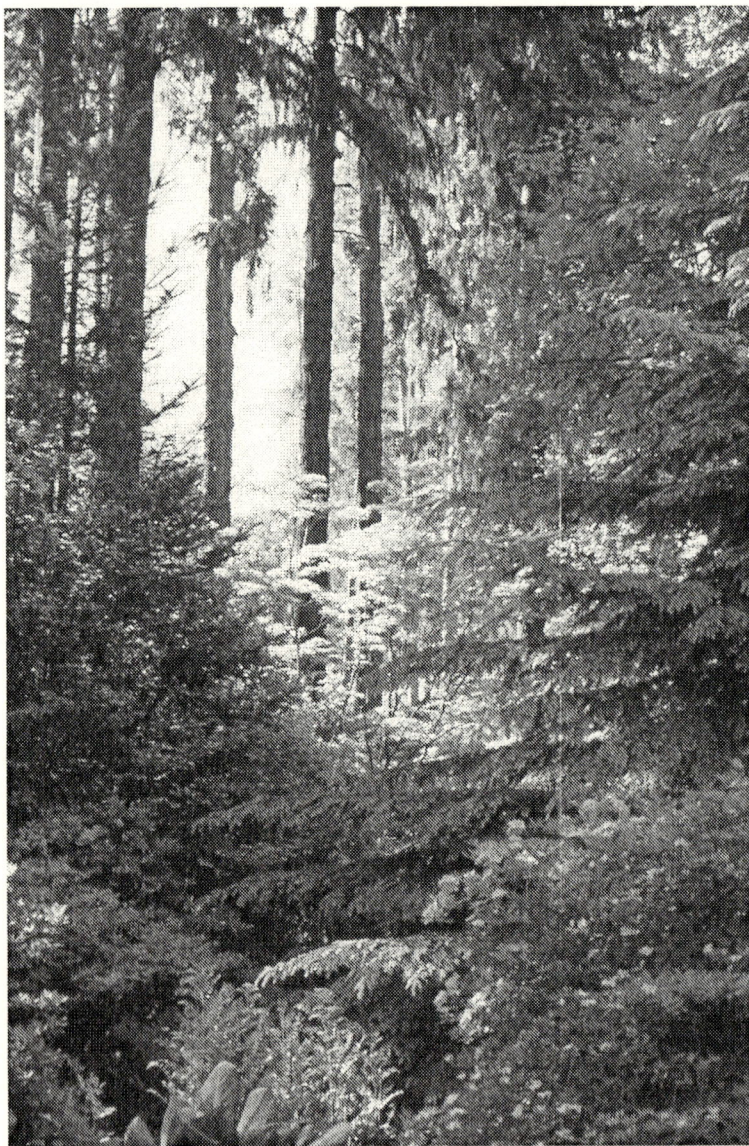

Forest within impressive landscape garden, Bodnant Garden, N. Wales, 5/94

VOICE CALLING IN THE WILDERNESS (1996?)

Sometimes I feel
like a "voice calling in the wilderness"
gushing forth such eloquent verse
and song with none of my own kind to hear,
but only my more cosmopolitan kind – the deer,
the owls, the spider, the locust, the songbird, the worm,
the tapir, the lion, and all God's humble creatures
– yet each with *being!*
Surely, universally related we all are,
and intercommunicating! – This I know!
... And no one is forgotten by/in
this hallowed *forest of love,*
not in/by each other and not in/by God!
And surely not by my very own self!

THOUGHTS UPON HEARING TERRY TEMPEST WILLIAMS (AUTHORESS OF "LEAP") TALK AT UNIVERSITY OF NEVADA-RENO (3/5/2001)

Thought #1
     Beautiful the realization that
under the ever watchful and caring
     hand and consciousness of God,
nothing and no one can keep
     any one of us from fulfilling
his/her/its own special destiny
     in relationship to all.
Praise God!

Thought #2
     I found in life
that I was being buried
     under tons of apathy
and spite, shoveled upon me
     by my many enemies,
shoveling their indifference
     or downright hostility
as a grave digger
     shovels shovel-fulls of dirt
upon a corpse. But –Alas!–
     I am not a corpse as yet!
... As though I ever could be!
     Praise God! Oh! Set me free!

Thought #3
        Amazing how
we are all ever
        coming full circle
to one another!

TOWARD THE FIFTH DYNAMIC NOW! (2001, THE NEW MILLENNIUM

I hail the great Fifth Dynamic,
so referred to by Scientologist folk!
'T is woefully lacking amidst humanity today;
and the living planet's now direly threatened because of this!

Consider then the several dynamics
by which the individual identifies itself:
First, there is one's individual worldly attached *Self*:
I, me, yours truly.
Second there is the enfleshed, affectionately regarded Family:
parent, sibling, spouse, offspring, *et cetera*.
Third there arises the greater functional social Group
one's consciously incarnate in,
be it community or nation,
i.e. culture with shared values worldly interned.
Fourth's identifying with one's whole incarnate kind,
for us Humanity, *Homo sapiens*,
a.k.a. specieism: that into which so many people today,
in this or lesser dynamics
are so exclusively, perversely self-absorbed,
creating an imbalance that's become most horrid!

For the *Fifth Dynamic* takes us to a higher, nobler plane,
for it's identification is with the *Whole of Life*:
the plants, the animals, the decomposers, and other kingdoms,
all of which indispensably, in freely inter-balanced fashion
go together to make a world:
an ecosystem brightly co-evolving!

... Many spirits all the same in essence, yet
expressed in myriad evolved and evolving kinds,
          and all these wondrously interdependent,
intertwined in patterns
          exquisitely defined in Time
so that each ever learns and, in turn, teaches
          God's ever greater lessons! – Please!

          For each soul's challenge
ever one of increasing wholeness and perfection is;
          and each step along the way
is in a way duly opposite the former
          as well as the successor, throughout time,
just as with left then with right foot we prance forth,
          according to all experienced events,
all governed by Heavenly principles and laws
          that build and resolve us all,
including all kinds and all worlds,
          through all greater dynamics
unto that greatest which is:
          both in and consciously with God!
–Praise God! And Hallelujah! shout.

AN EARTH DAY PLEA (4/20/2003)

More massive monuments to Mammon!
Many miserable minions mundanely mastered!
And so few really caring enough to question.
And all the Rest of Life left listing.

And Man too ultimately
his own Worst Victim
upon this planetary ship of
human ignoring, ir-revering, and self-serving!
–When will this ever end?!
–Oh! Dear God! Can this ever change?!

EXPERIENCE (9/6/99)

Within the sacred realm
of ALL EXPERIENCE
is all Sacred, Whole, and Perfect Truth!
So –don't you see?–
we're all in this together,
in this great journey we call *life,*
in this great place we call *world!*
So, let us show one another
great reverence and due respect!
So let us do unto others
as we would have them
do unto ourselves.

TRUE REVERENCE (7/25/2003)

True *reverence for life*
involves learning to treat
life as *subject*,
not as mere *object*;
learning to discern it as holy spirit,
not profanely regarding the body only.
Truly so. And in this may God help us all.

HEAL THE EARTH (7/18/99)

Enlighten the attitudes of people,
make them more reverent for life,
more identified with the planet Earth
and for the *Common Good*,
and Thou will heal the Earth
–Dear God!–
and Thou shalt surely heal the Earth!
Praise God!

WHAT NEEDS TO HAPPEN TODAY! (2/8/2005)

Glimpsing God's Plan
becomes our inspiration,
through whatever medium/media,
or through none.

Today what needs to happen
is more Heavenly guidance,
less worldly fetishy!
We must
get back in tune, in touch
with our individual
and collective soul.
... Then
what needs to happen
will happen!

What needs to happen today
is more humility
on the part of Man
in relation to
all the Rest of Life
who share this world as home,
and our treating such
as venerable subject,
not mere object to possess
– and in turn to possess us!

There needs to be
a restoration of Harmony
in our attitudes and life styles

as these concern the Rest of Life.
There needs to be
a Great Setting Free
of each and every species,
a humble and respectful learning
on the part of Man,
to live as a carer for and as an integral in
All Life's Great Freedom
as the fulfilling
of God's Great Plan!

Then together
all the vast and variously evolved beings,
whose destiny with Earth is linked,
of all the vast and varied,
yet intercomplementary and interdependent,
forms and kinds,
shall together in uplifting harmony sing!

And all the Earth
this chorus shall uplift
unto a Higher Plane,
that "upon Earth as it is in Heaven"
shall more than a myth become,
for a Living Reality,
a Spiritual Ecology,
a most brilliant and rescued Culmination
of all that we have ever lived and shared and dreamed,
concerning each individual
and our common,
magically interwoven
Spiritual Evolution.

Then Heaven and Nature shall again
in glorious concordance sing,
as we in united consciousness uplift
our voice, our song,
our eyes, our ears,
our hearts, our minds,
to God Our Prize, Our End!

MAN'S PYRRHIC VICTORY OVER LIFE (EXAMPLE OF A POEM WITH CHORIAMBS) (3/22/2005)

World was once glorious, free,
'til Man came along with his greed!
What is now needed:
Apocalypse' Steed
whose Warrior with bright lance will sever Greed's head
in order all Earth's Life to save!

This now will happen
in remarkable ways
as Heaven displays
God's rule of fair justice and mercy
– provision for all!

By our own irreverence
Hangman's noose we have tied!
Possessed by possessions,
of Higher Laws we've lost sight,
those moral in nature
that to Heaven call out
– to God whose perfections
most surely judge us!

So let's show compunction,
repent of old ways,
regain our redemption
through Reverence for Life,
for for all Life's True Source!

PROOF TIME: TIME OF ANSWERING UP, RESPONDING (SWINBURNE'S FORM OF SAPPHICS POETRY) (4/29/2005)

I.
Strike the culprit! Be as a fearsome hero!
Rest not 'til your Hon'rable Goal's attained, for
what's the profit: lazy adrifting, sliding
... o'er abyss's ...

II.
... Ever deeper, full of more terror, horror,
consequence of your own wrong choosing, acting?
Extricating consciousness from these pitfalls
turns out trying.

III.
Now is time of crucial and fateful reck'ning:
whether we shall triumph or perish in the
higher sense. So let's be so keen and faithful
all past's lessons

IV.
To adhere to. Suff'ring but lovely species
are now pierced, extincting, so we are called up-
on to now be valiant and rectifying
mayhems once done.

V.
Bright's the Dawning just now a-breaking, glowing
o'er Horizon's promising onward future
view. So don't relinquish your inward vision,
upward motion:

VI.

Know your long-sought destiny rests assured, for
these are times that test our own true, fine mettle:
persevering we shall each reach our calling
—forth from Heav'n flung.

VII.

We are forth from ancient and deadly pitfalls
soon delivered, *if* we will only answer
God's great challenge *not* to make world false idol
but to God go.

VIII.

Each new step with care must be taken, woven:
all relations honored as threads within the
whole, the loom that's world and all universe as
well. Awake now.

IX.

None by God's forgotten, remains forsaken;
not one conscious spirit or soul shall perish
in the end, for we all together join: Per-
fection's Plan! Aye.

X.

Each one Indispensable sure is – this know.
Present we are now and forever have been,
will be, unique yet all the same. So free now
live and let live.

LIFE AND DEATH, LIFE'S MEANING

DIMENSIONS OF CONSCIOUSNESS: A POEM CONCERN- ING LIFE'S MEANING (SPRING, 2003)

So many dimensions of consciousness,
boxes contained within yet bigger boxes,
spheres: within yet greater spheres,
there out there, in here,
to be discovered are
by each and every one of us,
as by ALL of us together.
... Parallel universes, as it were, we are,
yet ever *one throughout* ...

Consider the vast and twinkling stars,
most of which: whole galaxies,
we see, we hear, from the surface
of home planet Earth,
in whose inner depths also
many mysterious secrets
yet lie to unlock their truths,
when Time and Fate:
the Hand of God reveals!

Correspondingly, so many dimensions of consciousness
each individual being – each one of us – passes through
by means of birth, by means of death,
and that which corresponds
in the higher world
to this our worldly life,
more precisely by means of
attachment and detachment,
including sex and violence,
refinement and again growing heavy,

and all such dramatic transitions,
  though there are those so peaceful,
and each with its own special
  yet interrelated reason
– yet with all this the cycle
  ever and again is reborn,
not just to cycle, but
  to spiral forth discovering ...

  ... Related at each moment,
as throughout all such,
  with each and every so called "other"
parallel evolving being unique,
  each a point of consciousness,
and one who shall not desist
  until it reaches the very Highest
Dimension subsuming all lesser ones
  ... and many a weaving back
and forth there is between, among.

  Each point of consciousness over Time
this Goal Sublime pursues.
  Oh! Great wonder of life, of world,
of World of worlds
  ... thus, to be *So Free,*
for, thus, to rise So High,
  Ever by grace and to the Glory Divine!

CYCLING (1995?)

Oh! To think of all
the people who are born,
then "max" out in life,
fade away and die,
lying down in their graves,
bones and flesh returning
to the cosmic cycling
of materials and energies
and their souls likewise
to the cosmic cycles of immortal Spirit.
Aye! 'T is a contemplation most magnificent!
Is it not?
Surely so it is. Praise God!
And Hallelujah! shout.

LIFE OR DEATH? (2/27/2001)

"Life or Death?" is a question
of where you place your attention,
     of where you fix your identity
and your heart's affection,
     of where you focus your mind.
So let this be upon
     God, the Perfect and the Whole,
not upon worldly transient states,
     ever imperfect and unwhole,
for these but serve
     to point to God
—whose name we do forever praise!

TWO THOUGHTS ON DEATH (3/12/2001)

Death is the great delusion!
And so is Birth!
Both the great appearing
and disappearing act are,
of the spirit into
and out of the flesh
and the world.
Be not by this trick fooled,
for the Godly spirit lives on,
neither created, nor destroyed!
Surely not. Praise God! Praise God!

... I recognize the distinctive relationship
between remorse and mourning,
for one must come to terms
with all one's worldly attachments.

LIFE (3/12/2001)

This I have learned about Life:
that inherent in the very continuum
    of Time we each experience
in our own unique, yet interrelated fashion,
    is the very composition of thought-feeling
that leads to TRUTH!

YOUNG (1995?)

The one
who can still look forward in life
to its better part,
or realization yet to come,
has not grown old but remains
ever so young,
no matter how many rounds the Sun
this Earth has flown
since one's present life's
birthing dawn.
Surely it is so.
Praise God! Amen.

Author as a child of 14 months.

A CHILD (3/8/2001)

I entered into this world
a child laden with noble sentiment,
    full of noble love,
for all my fellow spirits,
    in all the diverse forms of creation.
But many have been
    the harsh receptions
to my presence here,
    the cold shoulders and
the indifferent or down right mean
    treatments. Yet, I am not
bitter because of this,
    but through this have learned
all the more to confide
    in Heaven and in God,
for truly He has opened
    such vast and wondrous
vistas unto my animal and plant kin
    as well as unto my fellow man.
Truly so He has.
    Praise God! Amen. Amen.

YESTERDAY (WINTER, 2001)

Yesterday,
and the shadows of my memory
        are not shadows merely,
but very lights that
        do brighten my way!

... The Beatles' song of this title
        has a compelling unity,
touching familiar notes
        in many of us,
though four decades nearly
        have passed since
it was first sung
        by our bright companions.

—Yes, it is
        a song that lingers,
as all my yesterdays
        do linger on!
Yet, for this very reason,
        these are integral
to the here and now!
        I hear them still!
And for this very reason
        a pertinent, timely lesson,
they must bear!

PLAY OF OPPOSITES (2/27/2001)

I find the play of opposites in life:
dullness: sharpness, weakness: strength,
viciousness: virtue,
as this is experienced
in all possible ways
in this we call life,
as a necessary interplay
and being like that
great and fateful wheel
which moveth up and down,
forward and backward
– and for this very reason
goeth forth unto all perfection
and wholeness, unto God.
Truly so it rolleth forth
unto all Heavenly Restoration.
Praise God! Amen. Amen.

OF HALLOWEEN SUN AND PUMPKINS (10/96)

I write:
of Halloween sun and pumpkins,
     ... and learning to treat life with subtle art,
by asking that further question,
     in "polite" society seldom dared,
by mixing witches and sorcerers with priests,
     ghosts and goblins with incarnate ones,
by magical spells
     –by facing grim Death
squarely in the face
     and therein discerning a Parody of "life,"
even the humorous side thereof.
     But the joke's on us,
for we mortals are the butt
     that's just burned out,
the presumptuous stick
     that's just gone flat,
while immortal souls,
     those dearly departed,
behold our worldly attachments
     and the "death" to which
these inevitably do lead
     from just beyond the Veil
(of Earthly Delusion).
     For they wear no worldly
masks, as we mortals do,
     nor to these masks
themselves attach,
     neither inside nor out.
They seek not to hide
     in any way, shape, or form,

nor do they even generally try
       –though some may from time to time!
They fly on white witches' broomsticks
       high up into a moon-lit sky,
there at last to greet
       a dawning New Day
... and this mellowly glowing,
       Halloween sun
and all the marvelously varied "pumpkins"
       its light reveals
in magically arrayed hues
       of fantastic reds, oranges,
yellows, and goldens
       –and has a place here too
most majestic purple–
       one with the subtle art of
all God's holy spectrum
       that's all encompassing, all unveiling,
from out all the mists of Time
       (we all have lived),
revealing this world
       according to diverse lights,
according to all interweaved times,
       including this specially
wrinkled Halloween one,
       so as to grasp this
ever forward cycling Spiral
       that is the true Life
we live, we share,
       and ever have and
ever shall —Eternal!—
       including all countless critters wherever.
And by this I mean the spirits thereof.
       ... Aye! Here's a subtle
art worthy to describe!!
       Praise ye the all-radiant God!

ONE HATES TO DIE, A LOOSELY KNIT BURTONELLE (3/21/2003)

One hates to die before one's time
before the soul's very purpose Divine
for being here upon this plane
unique, in fact, indispensable has been fulfilled
and it's such a shame to see one's life's blood spilled
upon the dry desert sands of indifference

For the inspired genius of true Action
a.k.a. Relation,
the Completion shall not forever be denied
–Oh! Great, as yet unfulfilled Potentiality
within Each one of us as within All
Praise God! Forever and ever.

In life each individual ever
in one or another way comes to face
the consequences of his/her/its choices
and through this process we all come
face to face with our own true selves
however bitterly betimes and with each
further meeting this we are ever doing.
How extraordinary these quirky
appointments in time may seem
yet how very ordinary indeed!

You know that to recognize relations
wheresoever you may roam in a truly benign and inspired way
–Aye!– 't is to awaken so much that has
for far too long lain latent

but that still   shall have its day
even in this present dawning   now a-breaking
both without and within   all this called *life*,
all this called   *you* and *me*
and *she* and *he*   and *we*

TO THE DEARLY DEPARTED, AN APOSTROPHE (9/27/ 2003)

To you
who are yet with me,
    though perhaps not so much
anymore in the flesh,
    yet in part
and for this very reason
    all the more recognized
in pure spirit,
    for by my own self-
reflected mind and heart detected,
    yes, within Beingness'
ever greater dimension
    – greater than the mere physical world
and all that it contains
    or would contain,
I say:
    God bless and God speed
you on your way,
    and may the spirit of
true, for compassionate, Love,
    not just the worldly possessive kind,
ever guide us all on
    – there where we're finally bound,
to that Great Celestial Home
    upon which all
separate unique paths converge,
    as all the minds and hearts and wills
of all souls
    upon God's Holy
and Ever Living Truth!

RESTORATION (9/2/99)

Those happy times,
those happy places,
    and all the relations therein known,
so quickly dashed to pieces,
    by Time and Fate,
or so it seems
    —remember them well,
that they may be
    restored some day
within one or more
    of those many lives
which you have yet
    in store to live!

DESTINY (8/8/99)

One knows where
one's destiny has called,
    presently calls,
and in future times
    still will call;
to what lives yet to be lived,
    to what special roles: played,
to which future, present, and past loves
    – Oh! so precious these –
all to further realize.
    Oh! Wondrous spiritual life!
Ever by grace and to the glory On High!

QUEST (8/10/99)

The process of life in its deeper sense
is a quest for meaning,
truth, unity, interconnection,
beauty, wholeness and perfection,
in which is to be found
true fulfillment, happiness, joy, love.
This goes on
in the true life of
each and every individual,
consciously evolving being.
And it is my great joy
in this my present life
to speak through my writings
to the very heart and soul of such.
Praise God! And Hallelujah! shout.

ANIMATION (8/2/99)

All that bespeaks animation
bespeaks life's great truth,
    its abiding spirit,
not the mere physical machine,
    taken in and of itself!
Surely not!
    Praise God! And Hallelujah! shout.

DEATH (8/2/2003)

Aging and death
are figments of the
mortal view of life.
In truth we
all live forever,
ever have, do, and shall,
one in Space,
one in Time,
and, most of all,
one in Spirit
– Oh! Holy Spirit
all transcending!
Truly it is so.
Praise God! Amen.

HEAVENLY REASON (7/27/99)

Recognizing the Heavenly reason
for each new, as old, aspect of
worldly life, for each
new, as old, experience
– all aspects and experiences ever being
so perfectly interconnected –
one is restored in faith,
uplifted in inspired belief
unto the very Highest who is God!
Truly so one is.
Praise God! I say, Praise God!
And Hallelujah! shout.

ATMOSPHERE (7/25/2003)

Mystically aware
of the great atmosphere of Time
that surrounds
each spell of conscious attachment,
or detachment,
I become aware
of life's higher
sense and purpose,
meaning and glory.
Truly so I do!
Praise God! And Hallelujah! shout.

THE PURE, TRUE LIFE (7/18/99)

Be not confounded, oh! my soul,
that the ideal life
seems not to jive
with the worldly manifest one,
for the spirit of life
exists upon a higher plane;
and though all
manifest here below
is a consequence
of its spiritual cause,
still the wheels of causation
can at times most slowly grind.
So, just keep your faith,
your attention fixed
upon the great Divine within,
existing beyond
all the world of mere
external manifestation,
and that ever supercedes
and outstrips this,
for such is within the miracle
of the evolving spirit,
who in ever more
perfectly awakening
consciousness does move,
that whole transformed
worlds of the future
become effected through
the wondrous powers
of our own true dreams,

visions, Heavenly inspirations
that are life's true work
and that especially go on within
one's own truest, for inmost, self,
whom the world cannot touch.
Truly not.
Praise God!
Praise God!

DEATH (7/14/99)

This I've learned about worldly life:
that death at last brings peace,
        and that there is a great beauty
then that arises from each
        life that's been lived,
experienced upon the manifest plane,
        as it resolves itself
with all that's come and gone
        before in past time,
and so goes on to
        that ever greater
resolution in times future,
        until all that has been written
also has been experienced, lived,
        and, so, its true meaning
fully learned, appreciated
        – every by grace
and to the glory of God!

AUTUMN LEAVES (A DODITSU) (10/24/2004)

Autumn leaves so cool and fresh,
about them there's a hint of death,
as owl hoots weirdly nearby
Paradoxic'ly.

LIFE'S PAUSES (2/12/2005)

It is in life's pauses,
one of which is so-called death itself,
that we are given time to reflect upon
that which we have just lived
and, so, then prepare ourselves for
the next wave:
our next new, more perfect life.
Praise God!

NOT FOR GRANTED — LIFE! (3/2/2005, DEDICATED TO MY DEAR MOTHER ALICE ON HER 92ND BIRTHDAY)

The character of each one
is vast and deeply drawn!
And there's a meantness in all this
– in each appointment, hers or his!
And all this hails the Dawn!

How many times one looks at life
as if there's no true sense,
but taking time to feel, reflect,
discovers promise, truth inflects
– reanimates credence!

Take not for granted any being!
We all are here as one!
In spirit we do ever share
life's wondrous purpose, meaning, dare!
And God shines as our Sun!

His lessons come in many forms,
in places and in times,
in meant encounters with all kin,
as music comes from out the din,
dischord transforms to rhymes!

And each pure soul has grace unique
– such wonders to perform!
O'er all the ages – many lives
and loves and deaths – being forth still strives
– *Creation to Transform!*

INDIVIDUAL EXPRESSIONS

THE BODY (3/13/2001)

The inherent logic in the body
as an adaptation for
    survival in this world
is beautiful to behold,
    for something more that just
physical survival
    and reproduction is involved.
Yes! Something more,
    and which no mere thing is,
and that all things subsumes.
    – Oh! Holy spirit
evolving back from the Fall
    and unto God!
Praise God!

FEATURES (2/23/2001)

What unique and special experiences
your features sculpted have
...your own unique and special knowledge,
elicited from out your own
true inner depths
Of ALL POSSIBILITY AND TIME?!
Ask of yourself and each other
this question well, oh! my soul,
that you the soul-smothering
veil of worldly delusion
may pierce!
For thus you'll perceive beyond,
for so conceiving.
Praise God! Amen. Amen.

AURA (1995?)

Each place has its own special aura,
or vibration, as does each person,
        each animal, each plant.
Yet none are separate!
        No nation stands apart!
No continent can
        within itself be contained!
For we all props
        to one another are;
and out of our
        very relationships
do fashion our identities.
        Oh! Sacred Forest
of kindred spirits,
        ancient in Time,
yet ever renewing,
        ever rebirthing,
ever young!
        Praise God! Amen. Amen.

INDIVIDUAL UNIQUENESS (9/21/2000, 52ND BIRTHDAY OF AUTHOR)

        Each soul decides
for him/her self
        which route to follow
according to the inner wisdom
        of his/her own true
heart and mind.
        He/she knows
what karmic debts
        he/she has to pay
and wherein his/her
        own unique destiny
does lie,
        one unique,
yet, paradoxically
        of indispensable relation
to that of all fellow souls,
        for this by dint
of a very individual and
        Divinely appointed uniqueness!

TRUE DEFINITION (8/7/99)

Being without a friend,
I learn to appreciate
        the true definition of "friend."
Without "love," as the world calls it,
        I learn to appreciate again
the true meaning of *Love*.
        And so it is
with all aspects of life:
        virtue, strength, intelligence, wisdom:
we learn the better to appreciate these
        from their outward absence,
for then we as individuals
        must call upon
our own inner selves
        in order to supply
these absolute necessities
        for the sustenance of life
—for then wondrously, miraculously,
        we find these to lie *within*.
Truly so we do
        Praise God! Amen. Amen.

PIONEER (8/2/99)

Be a pioneer in spirit,
searching out new perspectives
of universal truth,
that all may gain
by your daring.
Likewise do not refrain
from following in those times
when similarly you are led.
Praise God! I say, Praise God!

TRUE POSSESSION (8/3/99)

What greater possession
hath any man
than his own inward self
and experience,
such as makes us all equals,
though each following
his/her/its own unique way,
leading both to the
realization of one's own true self
and to that of all others,
all ways converging
upon the self-same
Truth Divine
throughout the whole eternity
of our becoming.
For such is life!
Truly so it is.
Praise God! I say, Praise God!

BRILLIANT SELF-IMAGE (8/2/99)

People fashion
their own self image around
many things,
but the Greatest Truth,
and all life's motion
towards this Wholeness and Perfection,
is ever testing these
transcient identifications,
or self images.

So it is best
to be aware of the process
and to seek to recognize as real
only that which is perfect and whole,
regardless of how
imperfect or unwhole
may be your and others'
current realization of such.
— Surely only the very best
shall in the end be attained
and give us true
and lasting Peace!

CHANNELER (7/31/99)

Be ye a channeler
from the ever
higher Heaven, oh! my soul,
unto this world
where you find yourself in body,
that an uplifter
you may be
and not a degrader;
a blessing,
and not a curse!
Surely so be ye!
Praise God! And set me free!

HAPPENING (7/27/99)

If you would know
the true happening of life,
look within
your very own self.
Praise God!

KNOWLEDGE OF THE SOUL (7/17/99)

To possess knowledge of the soul
and knowledge in relation to the soul
is more valuable
than all mere worldly life
and its offerings,
but perceived in relation to the immortal soul,
this same worldly life
takes on enhanced meanings,
is revived, for known in relation
to its own true and transcendent cause,
its Heavenly super-nature
– all in relationship to God!

AVOID WORLDLY MANIPULATORS (7/17/99)

Be not a mindless,
heartless, will-less puppet
    of the vested moneyed interests
who have little interest in your soul
    and its purpose for being here,
but only look shamelessly
    to their own worldly
self-aggrandizement!
    Be not so beholden,
but rather take stock within
    yourself and in all
that God has given you!
    In other words, stand up,
be brave and free and pure,
    for this is the way to life
—all else death is. Praise God!

STRIVE (7/17/99)

Strive to develop
sensitivity to life's
higher cause and meaning
that you may become
pure in heart
by questioning your motivations
and outlook upon life
that, thus, ye may learn to see
and in all ways
to perceive God.

UNITY, UNIVERSE, AND RELATION

A CHALLENGE CALLED *RELATION*: A QUASI-SONNETTELLA (AUGUST, 2001)

You know that Vain Science makes a "Religion"
out of arrogant Materialism,
and Thoughtless Technocracy to this does join
to bring Man Up, but put Life Down – Bad Schism!
– Yet Life's True Story's not so falsely written,
for something Greater from the Heart does dawn,
for within a Greater Tapestry knit in
our fine lives have been – and are yet still drawn,
according to a challenge called *Relation*
– by High Order of Love's Plan: **PERFECTION!**

THE MANY AND THE ONE: A PRAYER (APRIL, 1999, LA BONITA, SUCUMBIOS, ECUADOR)

I write a prayer,
about *The Many and The One!*
And, you know,
there's now Six Billion,
souls incarnate in human form
upon this beautiful,
but much fraught Earth!
And that's not counting
all the other souls who
in other diverse forms
are wrought.
Yet, you know,
however arbitrary worldly barriers
seem to be imposed
between and among us all,
as Heaven knows,
according to God's Perfect Law,
we all ever
One in Spirit are!
... And those relations
seemingly the most impossible
and remote
to our limited
mortal view of life,
in fact,
the most beautiful become,
for these correspondences
are the most Eternal,
the most Sublime!

THE SUN

(from Downer, Craig C. 1981. *Spiritual Evolution: A Book on Reincarnation and Evolution*. Page 102. Vantage Press, New York. Copyright by the author.)

In the midst of smothering darkness,
in all its holy starkness,
there burns a holy light,
kept ever by His might.

– Yet, though it be night,
't is dawn to me,
holding no fright,
but ecstasy!
There is a faint light,
all-permeating as Divine Love,
which sublimes to a height,
this world to the far home of the Dove!

In this dawn I want to awaken,
my eternal desire, constantly!
I want to be taken,
there, to home, to be free!
Where everyone is one,
a Glorious Sun!

TOUCHING (2/24/2001)

   Each touches ALL,
and ALL touches each.
   Such is the great,
interfused reality of Life,
   as ever onward we evolve,
self perfecting and thereby perfecting all
   who with us evolve
...that is in Time
   this process of recovery
of all that was lost at the Fall,
   this reawakening to
that great and *Glorious Perfection*
   that ever is and is Life's Truth!
Truly so. Praise God forsooth!

FELLOW SOUL (3/13/2001)

See each fellow soul,
as well as yourself,
in his/her/its
present condition
as integral to life's
great evolving story,
as not limited merely
to certain known
present and past states,
but as ever moving
unto its own,
and all our shared,
Perfect Realization,
as ever Forth out of Darkness
and into the Heavenly Light
that looms we all do go,
back from the Fall
and gloriously unto God.
Praise God!

THREADS (3/3/2001)

      Beautiful is the realization
of those long lost threads
      of time and experience
one once lived
      then seemingly forgot,
as these weave back,
      themselves again knot
into one's conscious life,
      as they present themselves once more
like long, lost strangers
      and for reasons beyond mere mortal law.
Truly so. Praise God! Praise God!

THE UNIVERSAL RELATION (3/2001)

Contemplating the ***universal relation***
wherever I do roam,
I think of ***Love***
and all it ***means!***
Considering all
the vast ***possibilities***
that unfold
throughout the whole of Time,
I am transported
beyond just this one
mortal experience
unto that **Greater Life**
all these tiny lives **subsumes.**
Yes, I think of
the ***True and Universal Love***
that awaits ***both me***
and us.
Truly so I do.
Praise God! And Hallelujah! shout.

THOUGHTS ON UNITY (3/10/2001)

Whether we like it or not,
or choose to recognize,
        the great sublime fact
of life is that
        we are all ever
one in spirit,
        one in the great transcendent,
Heavenly dimension. And even
        the physical realm,
which is the spirits' effect,
        or manifest expression,
teaches us this Great Truth,
        as in all Space and in all Time,
and by all types of things
        and manifest relations,
our sublime UNITY IN SPIRIT
        is proven. Truly so it is.
Praise God! Amen. Amen.

        ... Take the experience of life as it comes, oh! my soul!,
for though there appears to be
        a trillion, trillion, trillion, trillion, trillion,
individual souls in the Universe according
        to the exterior view of life,
in Truth, we all ever
        ONE IN SPIRIT are,
all in relationship to God.
        And this is the only,
sane view of life to have.

... True happiness in life
is learning to appreciate what comes one's way,
        for its universal fitting and Heavenly
meantness, or intent. Now,
        this amounts to
not taking life for granted!

... Beautiful is the remote correspondence
between and among all similar and seemingly
        dissimilar kinds: of mountains, of oceans,
of plants, of animals,
        of relatively impure and pure of conscience spirits
– and we are all this or have been or will yet be –
        of beings wherever, whenever, whomsoever,
and of whatsoever manifest form and behavior.
        Truly so magnificent this is.
Praise God! I say, Priase God!

TRANSITION (4/15/2003)

Each seething sunset slipping away
such a soothing significance portrays:
the end of this day's special dream,
the beginning of this night's,
as Poe's "silken, sad, uncertain ... curtains" fall
and Heavens again alight
with myriad twinkling stars
and galaxies so far out,
one has to reach very deep within
truly to know them!
Praise God! Amen.

CONNECTIONS (9/14/99)

   Subtle connections
exist *in spirit*
   between and among
all our diverse lives
   that, though often
seemingly unconnected,
   yet, in truth,
are always interconnected,
   and this in so many, many ways,
concrete and subtle,
   now apparent or now unrecognized,
and that all mutually complemental
   shall ultimately be judged,
for known—for lived! Praise God!

Five-year-old Salasacan maiden, Salasaca village, Tungurahua, Ecuador, 1997.

FACES (9/1/2003)

      Reminiscing upon all the places
and all the faces
      I have known,
by some magical blessing,
      these coalesce as one,
bringing me alive,
      prompting me to face
those future faces
      and places and times
that I shall yet know
      – and with such bright eyes
and such keen ears, *et cetera!*
      Praise God!

TAKING STOCK (8/23/99)

Look not with jealousy upon others,
but rather take stock in
what God has given you
throughout all times;
and know that we all
related are in life's
great and universal becoming.
For truly it is so.
Praise God! I say, Praise God!
And Hallelujah! shout.

UNITY (8/16/99)

There is a unity to life, world
such that each event, experience, expression
is universally recorded,
registered with all places, times,
and, most of all,
fellow spiritual ones.
And for this reason
there is no escaping
our responsibility
to one and to all,
including to each one's
very own true self.
Truly such unity there is.
Praise God! And Hallelujah! shout.

SPIRIT MIRRORS (8/8/99)

Each fellow being
is a mirror of yourself,
        showing forth to you
that same essential
        spirit you are and who
one with very universal existence is,
        the discoverer and knower
– the realizer of truth!

THE PART AND THE WHOLE (8/7/99)

Each part depends upon the whole.
The whole depends upon each part.
Each part is indispensably related to
each and every other part.
Each one is inseparable from the whole.
All related is,
ordered according to
very highest priority.
Godly spirit is Highest Truth.
All that is taken
as existing apart from Godly spirit
is misconception, perversity – the worldly lie!
This know and go free
to rise up on High!
Surely so do.
Praise God! And Hallelujah! shout.

MUTUALISM (7/31/99)

We do not live
to the denial, or put down
of one another,
but, rather, to the confirmation
and uplifting thereof
– ever by grace
and to the Glory of God!

ATTACK (7/19/2003)

To attack any fellow spirit
is to open oneself
for counterattack.
This is logical.
The resolution will ever
involve damage and healing to both sides,
not just the one
first attacked.
And thus it is
that we'll both
be the better off for it.
Praise God! And Hallelujah! shout.

RELATED (7/17/99)

      Each life is ever related
to each other life.
      All lives form
a great togetherness.
      Never forget this,
oh! my soul
      ... the interconnections,
how related we all are
      to each other
and how all in life tends
      to the very greatest of all ends,
in truth, a return to the "beginning",
      unto the very *Source Divine*!
Praise God! I say, Praise God! Amen.

OPPOSITE POINT OF VIEW (7/12/99)

To the vulgar way of viewing life,
the soul of life is worthless;
in fact, the less
soul-realizing souls the better
from their dark and dense
and unloving point of view,
caught in a fetish of sin.
But to the spiritually enlightened soul,
all the very opposite is true;
and this is, indeed, the truth!
Praise God! And Hallelujah! shout.

WITH THE WHOLE (2/8/2005)

Ever strive
to identify with the whole,
not just the part,
of life
– of beingness –
oh! my soul,
whoever you may be,
that both you and we
together may rise,
ever by grace
and to the glory On High!

THE WORLD, SOCIETY

MICROCOSM: MACROCOSM (3/9/2001)

In the microcosm,
the macrocosm is prophesied.
And, so, in each episode of Time,
the Whole Story of Time
prophesied is!
And even so, in the life of each soul,
is inherent the life of all souls! Praise God!

ELEMENTS (2/28/2001, READ AT SHUMAKER COLLEGE, UK, SPRING, 2004, BY XIOMARA NAVAS-CARBO)

All the elements for Perfection
are before us in the present,
    but we each must learn
to recognize how they rightly
    fit together, in what
just juxtaposition and proportion,
    wondrously symmetrical as pertains
to all aspects of Creation.
    – And for this reason,
there is **Time**!
    Truly so there is.
Praise God! I say, Praise God!
    Amen.

SOCIETY (2/26/2001)

A society is characterized
as much by what it ignores
        as by what it recognizes.
And often what it ignores
        is the greater portion
of God's Whole and Perfect Truth!
        So just take care, oh! my soul,
to, in pure honesty
        – that is the spirit of Love –
toward this Pure and Holy Truth
        go forth,
for thus are you free,
        ever by grace
and to the glory On High!

IMAGINE (8/2/2003)

Imagine a world
free of violence and lust,
full of mutual helping
and true love,
a world whose inhabitants
believe in themselves,
which is to say,
in their own spiritual essence,
and where the myth
of materialism
has been thoroughly dispelled.
Aye! Surely 't would be
such a great world, indeed!
Surely so it would.
Praise God! I say, Praise God!

PARASITE (7/29/99)

As mankind continues
to over-populate and over-pollute the world,
        to graspingly and grubbingly
parasite its resources,
        to emulate and glorify
his/her own creations,
        while ignoring the inherent spirit
in all *the rest of life*,
        and the wise ecological system
anciently coevolved among
        all diverse kinds
he/she only sets him/herself up
        for his/her own worst victim
to become! Surely, truly,
        none of this the
Light of Day shall stand!
        Priase God! Amen. Amen.

Iguazu Falls from Brazilian side with inner glow, mid-morning.
10/2004

A SHRINE (7/27/99)

Consider the world a shrine,
place where so many lifetimes
and so-called "death times,"
cycles of fleshy attachment
and detachment have been lived
by myriad souls so diversely evolved,
yet ever so intrinsically related.
– A holy shrine, I say,
place of suffering and joy,
of growing pains and happy triumphs,
according to the diverse
stages in which one's involved
and all mediated from Heaven on High!

Surely so consider ye
      this life, this world: this *school*
... this evolutionary progress,
      that is at times a struggle
at other times a graceful flow,
      but which always on
to the very highest of goals
      does go,
ever by grace
      and to the glory
of very God on Highest High!
      Praise God! I say, Praise God!
And Hallelujah! shout.

ROT (7/26/99)

       Thank God for rot and rottenness,
that decline, death, and decay
       may pave the way
for new and better times
       filled with seemingly "old" souls
now made "new,"
       for recycling on this Earth,
as, indeed, upon other meant
       planes of dwelling.
Thank God then
       for the clearers of the way,
even betimes for those
       who kill or let themselves be killed,
as for the decomposers
       who themselves then in turn
killed or died and decomposed are.
       …and "turn the soil."
Truly so. Thank God!

NEGATIVE REACTIONS (7/22/99)

Negative attitudes
result in negative reactions!
When the souls of mankind
ruthlessly put down
the *Rest of Life* with whom
they share this planet Earth as home,
they cause horrible negative reactions
against themselves in future times,
that they might learn
true reverence for life
– all in relationship to God!

WORLDLY MONUMENTS (7/19/99)

There's many an external
monument created
in the name of communication,
but none can compare
with a single inspired moment
experienced by any soul,
nor can any such worldly monument
alone and by itself this command.
Surely not. Praise God! Amen.

MONEY (7/17/99)

People are conditioned today
from the time they are born
to the time that they die
to believe that money is truth
and worldly possession is reality,
when both alike
are utter lies,
for those who put their faith,
and trust and effort
in these end up
empty and depraved,
and finally dead,
dead in spirit, if not in body dead.
–Surely none of this
the Light of Day shall stand!
Praise God!

WORLDLY SUCCESS (7/17/99)

There's many a worldly success
rich in material possessions,
    so called "high" in society,
yet who's become
    a dismal moral failure,
spiritually bankrupt,
    for disattuned and out of touch, *et cetera.*
So envy not
    such as him or her,
for there's so much
    more to life than this!
Praise God!

BREATHING, DRINKING, EATING (7/12/99)

Breathing the air,
we communicate with all the atmosphere!
Drinking water:
with all the lakes, the rivers and the streams,
the clouds and the oceans!
Eating food, we communicate
with all the rocks and sands,
plant and animal bodies.
And through these
means of communication
we are also inspired,
through the all combining
Living Presence
– whose source most Heavenly is!

BEWARE MUNDANE AUTHORITY (7/12/99)

Learn the art
of staying free
from worldly dictatorships
especially those vicious,
oft cleverly disguised,
mundane authorities
who would seize
hold of your heart and mind and will
through oft subtle and devious ways.
Be pure enough
to slay them with
the Holy Sword of Truth,
brought back to life
within your consciousness
and higher conscience,
by grace of God. Praise God!

GEOMANCY (7/12/99)

Vibrations
of different places or regions
　　　are powerful! There are
special messages in these,
　　　written in the very ethers
of Time. I think here
　　　of ancient Egyptian lands,
of holy Israel, of soaring Andes,
　　　even of my present life's
native land of Nevada,
　　　mystic and austere,
and so become
　　　ever so appreciative
of this planet Earth,
　　　all of whose diverse
regions are necessary
　　　to the whole globe,
even as a perfect sphere
　　　unites all of its parts,
each region offering
　　　each unique, yet universal soul
some special lesson,
　　　some unique point of perspective
indispensable for its advancement
　　　as well as an opportunity
to uniquely contribute, according to the time.
　　　Truly so I do.
Praise God! I say, Praise God! Amen.

FULL DECK (2/8/2005)

Life is like
a full deck of cards
in that it takes
all distinctive characters
to make up a world,
and what's more:
a spiritual dimension;
and we each
not only hold,
but *are*
one of these
ever vitally related cards.
Praise God!

THOUGHT, ETHICAL LIFE, GOD

```
        *
       **
      ****
     ******
    ********
   **********
```

CHRISTMAS POEM 2002

Lest we forget
Life has many Great Wonders for us yet
in store, as Time ever reveals.
– Have Faith and be of Good Cheer!
God has promised these to us,
each according to its time,
but we must keep our promises to Him,
of a faithful, hoping, truly Loving Heart,
ever striving on,
one Bright with Heavenly visions,
and to these True and
not sin-given!
Praise God! Amen. Amen.

```
      *******
       ******
        ****
         **
          *
```

MY GOD'S BLUE BLISS (A TETRAMETRIC RUBAIYAT, 5/26/2001)

I find myself now fifty-two,
a lonely wanderer so blue,
or so 't would seem but for my muse,
one wholly real as me or you!

... My muse in whose most varied moods,
sometimes excited, sometimes soothed,
my heart, my mind, my will bedight,
according to some Higher Truths!

Now speech and music, image, sound,
within my conscious life resound!
– Oh! Lord! Now how my spirit soars
in conscious these to come full round!

... Time's coalescing puzzle this,
no piece of which I'd ever miss,
for I behold with future sight,
solution Full – my God's Blue Bliss!

TO PLUCK A THOUGHT – AN ORVILLETTE (1/30/2003)

To pluck a thought out of thin air,
to plumb a feeling deep within:
of what avail I ask you now?
'T is soul's fine work, one, Oh!, so *Fair*!

To pluck a thought out of thin air,
to soar to heights, defy the world,
by means deemed strange – don't ask me how!
'T is soul's fine work, one, Oh!, so *Pearled*!

To pluck a thought out of thin air
unravels myst'ries so profound,
such phases one with a great *Pow*!
'T is soul's fine work, one, Oh!, so *Crowned*!

To pluck a thought out of thin air
brings one *to face oneself* as well.
– Can you not see?! 'T is *Plan Divine*!
'T is soul's fine work, one, Oh!, so *Belle*!

TEMPTATION (7/11/95)

The easy, tempting way of vice
becomes a slippery road to Hell,
    as the more one moves along,
the faster one descends
      ... as many a poor soul should attest!

EXAMPLE (3/14/2001)

Be an uplifted,
inspired example yourself,
oh! my soul, of
all the great, positive,
virtuous affirmation
in and for life,
for, thus, your own
true living example
shall positively effectuate,
gloriously dramatic change
throughout for beyond the world.
Praise God!

GOD: RESTORER OF THE DOWN-FALLEN (1998?)

After one's choices for sin
have made a ruin
of one's current cycle, or life,
God picks up the pieces thereof
and puts them back together again.
And for this reason
we justly call our
ever living, ever loving God:
the Very Greatest of All,
the Supreme, the Most High,
the One who never fell
and, so, who never fails,
the Most Worthy of Our Love,
the Most Faithful and True
– and so must we be to Thee!

ADVANCEMENT (9/1/99)

No true advancement
is ever made by putting others down,
though it appears this way
to the worldly point of view,
for rather,
all the very opposite is true!
Advancement is made
by lifting others up,
sincerely and out of
worldly disinterested
love for this fellow self,
and because one perceives
the special *Divine within*
each special soul embarked upon
its special way ... and then
in this brave act
of virtuous giving, relating,
one oneself uplifted is
... though all love is
true giving alone
for love's sake alone,
and by the same token
a loving in receiving
another's true love for one.
Praise God! Amen. Amen.

REPROOF ((8/26/99)

      Time is vast;
and there is ever the reproof
      for every rash,
worldly excess
      and overblown claim,
as each and every soul
      shall surely come to learn.
Praise God! Amen. Amen.

THE GODLY SPIRIT (8/24/99)

Those who speak of
the mystical reality of life and world,
        speak of that which
beyond mere tangibles is.
        They speak of the Holy Essence,
the Godly Spirit,
        that which is known within
and corresponds to
        the *withinness* of all things
– the Heaven within –
        the finding of oneself in all,
the right reading of all symbols,
        the inner reviving!
This pursuit the piercing of
        the veil of worldly delusion is.
It is the true
        Road to Salvation!
But to get on this
        holy road one must
be willing to make sacrifice
        of all worldly delusion
and sinful attachment.
        This is the noble way.
But each one of us must
        decide for him/her/it-self.
Praise God!

        ... So be unbound by mortal views!
Rise, oh! my soul, to highest heights,
        there, life's Eternal panorama to behold
– so beautiful, so joyous, so full of Love!

279

VISION (10/7/99)

  The experience of life
can be heart-rendering at times,
   but ever it is my vision of God
that keeps me going on.
   Truly so it does.
Praise God! Amen. Amen.

NOT IN VAIN (8/18/99)

Know this, oh! my soul:
your soul life
        is *not in vain*!
So just take care
        not to become
hung up on
        worldly false values,
so that you may
        learn to value
the inner life you lead
        and that stores up
such great treasures from Heaven,
        which is to say, from God
...unique treasures upon which
        all the world depends,
as upon your discovery of them
        – then learn to appreciate
the same in everyone,
        even those seemingly
most different from yourself.
        Surely so do.
Praise God! I say, Praise God!
        And Hallelujah! shout.

LOVE

THE GOAL: A POEM ABOUT LOVE (1/24/2001)

Beware of where you place your **heart**
that disillusion yours be **not,**
this bitter fruit you reap to **death**
because of *worldly fetish* – **No!**
But keep your heart so fixed upon
that *Bright Star* that does still to **dawn,**
that **Star** which though so far unreached,
yet still touches us with its Light!
In it you will find a sure *guide*,
that in its steadfast **glow** your *quest*
shall ever draw ye *nigh to God*
for this Light is His own true Love
—our true and perfect **Goal Above!**
Praise God! I say, Praise God! Praise God!

MAN AND A WOMAN — A KELLY (10/30/2000)

A man and a woman
attracted, no one can
        divide, part asunder,
when married they're "made one"
        so far as this world-hemmed,
long life is concerned!
        —Yet those of a higher,
more subtle, fine knowledge
        in Love see more than
mere mortals attached!

THE SEA BECKONS (AN EXERCISE IN IDENTIFYING WITH THE OPPOSITE SEX) (5/15/2002)

"Widow Maker"
some call the Sea,
    but bristly brine
and salty spume
    and blue horizons,
vast and far,
    remind me of
my precious Love
    and shall so long
as I'll reside
    beside these lovely,
deathly waves
    Alas! – that stole
my Love away!
    Yet these give life
as well in me:
    so much in them
I see, perceive,
    for my Beloved's
presence here
    to me does sing,
is seen and smelled
    and tasted still
– exquis't'ly felt! –
    in salty brine
and fresh, sea air,
    in Images
conjured up

from dashing surf
– BENEATH! –
and dreamy clouds
– O'ERHEAD! –
as in ALL this
Land-Sea-Sky Match!
... And in the very
stone cliffs His Face is wrought!
... And in these very
rhythmic waves,
there is a Pounding of
my Heart's own Song,
commingled with One
now sailed Beyond
– where too I'll soon be bound!
Praise God! Amen.

LOVE (3/3/2001)

      The experience of Love,
in this life and world,
      a Taste of Heaven
most surely is
      – this pure spiritual
communication of unity
      and caring,
no matter how great
      the difference between/among
      our creature form
or worldly situation,
      for a Higher Relation
most truly this is
      —ever by grace
and to the glory of God!

THE LAMB OF LOVE – AN ONDA MEL (4/20/2001)

       Gentle lamb, cradled in Christ's arms,
Adoringly,
       Confidingly,
– Surely you will come to no harm!
       Bright spirit uniquely shining,
Conceived Above,
       Pure child of Love,
– You're MORE than all world's defining!

..A LOVE (9/1/99)

There is a love
that goes deep
into the very roots
of our shared relation,
to that time
before the Fall,
before the taint
of sin and false idol
had blotted out
the holy consciousness
of that very greatest
and all-uniting,
most whole and perfect,
and, now, most restoring
Love of God!

HAPPY ... SAD (7/15/2003)

Sad, one becomes happy.
Happy, one grows sad again,
        et cetera, *et cetera*, according
to the great eternal rhythm,
        the sweeping melody
that carries one forth,
        and all with one,
and one with all,
        for ever so mysteriously
we related are.
        Truly so. Praise God!

LOVE (7/22/99)

Love is a wonderful phenomenon:
to experience it is to know
the very spiritual essence of life
and through this one's relationship to ALL.
Truly it is so. Praise God!

THE LIGHT (7/15/99)

The Light shineth *within*
and therefrom
shall not extinguished be!
It shines in each and every
individual soul,
in every heart and mind and will
and shall not be overcome
by the Darkness,
but shineth still;
no matter what has happened
–it will forevermore!
Truly so it shall.
Praise God! Hallelujah! shout.

DARKNESS? (10/18/2003)

      Darkness, oh! my soul,
is but the harbinger of Light;
      and, so, it is
with every seeming absence, or lack,
      for these, keenly felt,
do usher in
      the very Fullness and Love
of we all for each other,
      for of God!

FACT OF LIFE (2/09/2005)

The karma of loving attachment
is reflected in worldly life, or incarnations,
and our relations therein.
Forming attachment to a woman or man,
as the case may be,
is not as superficial
as many like to believe,
but carries on
in future lifetimes,
when one becomes
the son or daughter,
the mother or father,
of one's former lover.
And there is such great beauty
and wisdom and justice
in this higher
fact of life!
– And plenty of time for this!
Praise God!

TRUTH, UNIVERSAL PRINCIPLES, DIMENSIONS

THE TRUTH (8/7/99)

The truth abides
and no lie can effectively deny it!
Heavenly is the truth
– *all in relationship to God!*

THE THREE DIMENSIONS (8/2/99)

It is imperative
that we not only recognize
    the various dimensions,
but also rightly prioritize
    them unto the highest,
the most all-inclusive
    wherein lies
life's greatest, purest truth!

To wit: *Space* that is included
    and transcended by *Time*;
Time that is included
    and transcended by *Spirit*.
For, in final analysis, it is *Spirit*
    that is all life's greatest truth,
and, so, all the world's,
    and World of worlds,
for *Spirit* very Godly is!

OMNIPRESENCE (7/27/99)

The spiritually aware
perceive the spirit everywhere
and in all Time.
They know all life's
forms, animations,
perceiving in each unique style
a special spiritual state
and condition. This is
the art of perceiving life
that far transcends
the mere science
of superficial measuring
and describing such.
And all our conscious
journey of discovery
full of such art is.
Praise God!

PARALLEL (7/27/99)

There is between
one's thoughts and feelings
    and their progress toward truth
many a wondrous parallel
    in the externally manifest world.
This relation is one of
    cause and effect.
And this can work both ways
    when specially imbued
become these effects.
    Praise God!

ACTION: REACTION (7/22/99)

"For every action,
there is an equal
but opposite reaction"
applies as much to
inter-personal relations
as to inter-species relations
– that we all together come
to truly **Love One Another**
through our common
worship of God
– our most precious Lord God
whom we all share.
Praise God! Forever and ever.

FORMS (10/2003)

Forms are wondrous:
to see how they incorporate
all things into one
great design.
And so are all our lives:
these all relate,
connect to one another.
And as each one
purifies his/her
outlook on life,
so he/she begins
again to discern
the interconnecting lines,
the patterns and the forms, *et cetera*.
And the unifying plan, or design,
with its ever life-saving
meaning is brought home.
Truly so it is. Praise God! Amen. Amen.

SHARING (7/17/99)

What do we all share
if not Time?!
And if we all share Time,
we all share Space as well.
But most of all
it is *Spirit*
that we all share,
for Spirit unites us,
beautiful, transcendent Spirit,
that all Time
and so all Space
includeth and surpasseth.
Truly so it doeth.
Praise God!

SPIRITUAL MATRIX (7/15/99)

As spirits
we all together form
the spiritual matrix,
or context, for
each other's actions
in spirit,
which is to say,
in quintessential thought, word, and deed.
And no individual spirit
is without its
special universal effect.
Truly so. Praise God! And Hallelujah! shout.

ETERNITY, WONDER

ETERNAL SOUL (8/7/99)

Each soul goes on forever;
ever has been, ever is, and ever will be
one with all Eternal Truth.
And in this process called "living"
is Truth's rediscovery,
as forth out of Darkness
and unto Light one emerges,
back from the Fall
and unto God!
... Believe in this, oh! my soul,
whoever you are,
and you will be saved,
by the everlasting grace
and to the everlasting glory
of the Lord our most precious
God On High!

WONDER (7/31/99)

To grasp the wonder
of just one moment in Time
        is to glimpse all Eternity,
in essence. So look
        with heartfelt welcome
upon where you are
        right here and now,
if you would appreciate life,
        for lest you so learn
you will not appreciate
        any of it. For shame!

WONDERFUL (7/18/99)

Wonderful how
all our lives
ever related are,
for all our beings
from the same Source come!
To realize this
is such great liberation
from artificial barriers imposed,
from the worldly lies
unto God's Heavenly Truth.
Praise God!

BEAUTY: A CHANT (7/12/99)

      Beauty there is in death,
beauty there is in birth,
      because these miracles tell
of the soul's passage in and out
      of incarnate life
and force us
      to consider life's
higher meanings, its relation
      to Eternal Truth,
to God.
      Beauty there is in death!
Beauty there is in life!

MORALITY, ETHICS, JUSTICE, GOOD AND EVIL, VIRTUE

VANQUISHING EVIL (8/7/99)

Against seemingly impossible odds,
and when least expected by worldly smug
        vain types, you shall
vanquish over all sin and evil,
        all worldly darkness and lies,
by your very uplifted thoughts and feelings
        and willings to the Most High!
And your home shall become
        a most mighty sanctuary,
unassailable by the forces of wickedness,
        however these may surround,
a home invincible in the good,
        for a Heavenly channel,
pure and uplifted
        in and by God's pure
and perfect truth.
        While all profaned lives around
shall go down into the devouring
        flames of Hell, you shall
stand, oh! pure and valiant soul,
        and where none have stood
since before the Fail;
        and not just stand,
but further advance ye shall
        into God's ever beautiful and true,
Light of Salvation and Life and Love.

RIGHTEOUS (7/30/99)

A righteous life
is an unassailable fortress
that shall withstand
ALL the vicissitudes,
the tides and winds
of Time. Praise God! Amen.

HUBRIS (7/31/2003)

Let not worldly hubris
wax in your heart
and mind and will,
for it is an obscurer of such
and ever is cut
to the quick
by Time and Fate
and *Sacred Justice*!
Truly so it is.
Praise God!

THE SAINT (7/28/99)

Few people appreciate
the role of the saint
in society today.
Yet, it is verily
the highest of roles, as by
maintaining the conscious link
with Heaven such proves
a veritable life-saver
for all concerned.
And we are all related,
and for this reason
when the saint ascends
to higher conscious planes,
ones closer to God,
so all the world
likewise ascends,
for thoughts and feelings
have universally uplifting wings.
Truly so they do!
Praise God! And Hallelujah! shout.

VIRTUE (7/27/99)

He who
consciously possesses virtue
            possesses more than
all worldly wealth!
            He who
knows peace of mind
            and Heavenly order
together with priority of heart
            and nobility of enterprise,
or will
            has reached the objective
of all this worldly school.
            Truly so he has.
Praise God! I say, Praise God!

PETTINESS (7/22/99)

Pettiness is the enemy
of all noble, virtuous advancement,
        the "friend" of sin,
but sin ever proves
        itself to be
no one's true friend
        at all, indeed!

GIVING...RECEIVING (8/18/99)

Higher metaphysical law
teaches us that
in giving we receive,
hence the beautiful consequence
of generosity
... though we must give
out of love for the other,
out of identification therewith,
all in relationship to God.
Praise God!

CORRUPTION (7/17/99)

A "big head"
often corresponds
    to a small and petty mind;
a vain and worldly self-vaunting
    heart and will,
with all the abysmal
    corruption thereof!
Surely, truly,
    none of this thé
Light of Day shall stand!
    Praise God! Amen.

DECEIT (7/15/99)

Be not suckered in
by worldly enticements,
promises of paradise and joy
centered around earthly
possessions of the flesh
and the mere physical
realm of bodies and processes
taken in and of themselves,
and including the mundanely intellectual
knowledge thereof,
for what an utter lie these ever prove,
so terribly disillusioning
– what a horrible self-deceit!
Be not so deluded and deceived,
but rather look to all of life's
true and Heavenly Source
– all its great, transcendent spirit
in whole and perfect
relationship to God! Praise God!

COMPASSION (7/13/99)

Compassion
the very crown
of wisdom is,
the real proof
that one has
finally made the grade,
attained enlightenment,
risen free
from petty worldly attachment,
possessiveness, jealousy,
lust, false worldly values,
and all the other
ponderous weights
that hold any soul down!

LOVE OF JUSTICE (7/14/99)

Who loves justice
more than worldly life itself?
Who gives the righteous
joyful welcome?
The lovers of
higher spiritual truth!
The reverencers of life!
Such prove their mettle true
by standing up for what is good,
making all needed
worldly self-sacrifice.
Such will be welcomed
to their great
and sweet reward
in Heaven,
to receive a "well-done"
from God
after the final curtain descends
upon this their relatively brief
and fleeting worldly life.
Truly so they shall.
Praise God! And Hallelujah! shout.

LIFE'S HEAVENLY IDEAL, GOAL, PEACE

THE GUIDING STAR (7/31/99)

He who retains
the great overview of life,
relating this
one mortal experience with
all past and all future,
keeps on an even keel,
is not taken in,
keeps sight through insight upon
life's great and noble ideal
by which to guide him/herself,
as a ship's navigator
by some sure Star
– that surely shall not fail!
Truly it shall not.
Praise God! I say, Praise God!
And Hallelujah! shout.

INNER PEACE (7/27/99)

Be at peace with your inner self,
weaned from external distraction,
        harmonious within, feeling
full and happy and content
        in that blessed stillness
which is your Heavenly inheritance
        and everlasting place of refuge,
which nothing and no one
        merely worldly can
take away from you,
        for this is your
own special branch of Heaven
        that like any branch of any tree
to all other branches
        as to the main trunks
and *the Trunk*
        connected is.
... And it is in
        both the give and the take
that one knows and feels
        oneself not to be just a part
but the whole of all that is!
        All in everlasting
relationship to God!

HEAVENLY GIFTS (7/14/99)

       Never become
so caught up in
       worldly affairs
and preoccupations
       that you spare no time
to stop and think,
       meditate and reflect,
to know what's really
       going on in life,
to clear away
       the worldly confusion,
to receive
       the Heavenly perspective,
consoling insight,
       inspired directive.
Praise God! Praise God!

PERFECTION (7/12/99)

     The spirit of life,
seeing, hearing:
     in all ways sensing
imperfection,
     sets about to restore
perfection
     from that sublime
and inner sense,
     or image innate, or voice
that, or rather, *who*
     Divine most surely is !

LIFE'S PAIN AND JOY – FIVE CINQUAINS (4/12/2004)

Head ache,
dull, depressing,
makes me seek God's blessing,
and no more to take for granted
Virtue.

Wonder:
life forever
unfolds within each one.
There is no gain without some pain.
–How true!

Joyful!
The sun does rise
again to greet new day.
Another chance is given now.
–Thank God!

Who knows
what day will bring?
Some unique unveiling
for each one of us salvation:
Lesson.

A *Goal*
an inner light
reveals. Ancient promise
just now fulfilled, yet still points on
to God!

OVERGRAZING RECTIFIED BY GRACE – A BALANCE POEM (3/26/2004)

I find it most remarkable how man
o'erlooks the crux of major wrong!
Take overgrazing Earth
by hordes of cows
so forced,
coerced!
I ask just now
how can there be such dearth
of conscience, rev'rence pure and strong!
But it's my knowledge sure that we now can
face up to past mistakes and take a stand,
make bold our steps for change and long
to reestablish mirth
by sweat of brow,
remorse
–no curse,
but blessing!– how
among all kinds we forth
relating harmony will throng
the very gates of Heav'n –bright future Land!

REDEMPTION – A LAI POEM (2/2005)

A bright new lesson
for each life session
must come,
just compensation
for tribulation
which from
right's brave adoption
came as condition
– saved Mum!

TRUST, BELIEF, FAITH

TRUST (7/31/99)

    Those who put their
trust in the world
        shall taste death,
but those who believe
        in God's Heavenly Truth
concerning *ALL*,
        even this manifest
life and world,
        shall uplifted be.
– Truly so they shall.
        Praise God!
And Hallelujah! shout.

FOUNTAIN OF YOUTH (7/20/99)

       Look forward
with uplifted belief
       to the future,
for this is
       the secret of youth.
Praise God!

PATIENCE (7/18/99)

Those who bide their time patiently,
seeking to do God's will,
answering the Heavenly
calling for their life,
not seeking to rashly impose
a worldly corrupted will,
shall find themselves
most blessed
– and oft when least expected!
Truly so they shall.
Praise God! And Hallelujah! shout.

****

To Jennifer,
May the New Year
bring you many blessings —
spiritual friends and great
adventures. It is a special
joy to have you as my friend —
Love always,
Alice G. Downer

Printed in the United States
33652LVS00008B/49